I WAS SUPPOSED TO BE NOTHING
Memoirs of Storms, Sunshine, and Success

I WAS SUPPOSED TO BE NOTHING

Memoirs of Storms, Sunshine, and Success

by Toni Rain

Edited by Shanika Carter of
The Write Flow & Vibe, LLC

Toni Rain
Grand Rapids, MI

I was Supposed to be Nothing by Toni Rain

ISBN: 978-1-7329310-0-8

First printing 2018.

Printed in the United States of America by Michigan State University Libraries.

Toni Rain LLC Publisher
PO Box 7442
Grand Rapids, MI 49510

www.tonirain.com

Dedication

My nieces and nephews help give me the will to endure it all and to keep pressing forward. The love that I have for the children in my family is unexplainable. My heart just fills up to the lid when I think of them. Whenever I am around them, it's almost as if my entire soul lights up. They bring so much love and light into my life. They only see the good in me, and I only see the good in them. We play and talk just about every time that we hang out with each other. This goes for the infants as well. I'll talk their little ears off and they just watch and listen. I want the children to see, hear, and feel the love that I have and want for them. They can also say that I have never raised a hand to them. I use my hands only with gestures of love and affection when it comes to them. I personally don't believe in disciplining a child with my hands. I feel that my voice is enough. Besides, I know they will continue to respect me more if I only communicate with my voice. I don't want people to put their hands on me, so I won't do it with a child, especially when I see them as defenseless.

My personal time is so limited. This is a major issue that I often internalize. I want to spend so much time with my family, but I just have very little of it. I always feel like I am rushing through life. The majority of my time is balanced between being with my family, working, and enjoying social events; there is very little down time. I currently have 27 nieces and nephews; it's almost impossible to cater to each of them. I've learned that I have to spend time with them in groups. I recently decided to host events throughout the year for the children. I plan an annual tea party for the girls, and I have an annual game day party for the boys. I intend to have a yearly carnival for both the girls and the boys. This way, I'm able to see the majority of them at least a few times out of the year. I try to give them the experiences that I wish I had while growing up. Oftentimes, I say that I live my life backwards because I'm truly a "kid at heart" in my adult years. I read something along the lines of, "If you stop moving, then you'll stop moving." I looked at those words and told myself, If you stop living, then you'll stop living. I wanted to continue to live and be as youthful or "youth-like" as I possibly could. I want the children to know that I'll always love them no matter what. I want to leave them with some family history. I want to be a life example that life will give you lemons, but you must make lemonade or punch with those lemons. You have to keep pressing forward and onward. This book is not necessarily just for me but also for my family. It's for them to learn many keys of life and the keys and doors to success.

"Don't cry over the past it's gone. Don't stress about the future, it hasn't arrived. Live in the present and make it beautiful." - Author Unknown

Table of Contents

Introduction

As I put pen to paper, I sit here thinking, *Hmm, where should I start? So, do I do a tell-all book or fan fiction? Or even a fiction story?* Well, I'm the type of person who likes to speak what I call "all truth". It took me many years to figure that "all truth" was the thing that most people adored about me. Ever since I was a young child, I could remember people wanting to open up and share their stories with me. I absolutely love the fact that people feel comfortable talking to little ol' me. I guess people are like little water fountains, ready to let themselves flow down the stream we call life. Once the button on the fountain is pushed, that "water" gets to flowing on out. I am that special person that gets to push the buttons to let their pleasures, pain, questions, thoughts, etc. flow out. I'm their little helper in a sense. Other times, I look at myself as the mother of the universe. I'm willing to listen and help her children (all those who admire talking with me). Every person needs to let out their fears, tears, and thoughts to at least one person. I'm so delighted that I'm one of these people others can turn to. I've heard so many different stories about people's lives. The stories are sometimes unfortunate.

One story that sticks out to me like a sore thumb is about a little girl who was once molested by her father. The mother of the child had a disability that made it difficult for her to render to her daughter's protection. Now I don't know how long the molestation took place, but there was a lot of damage that had been done to this dear young girl. One of the most dramatic circumstances that occurred was that the father passed on a disease to this little girl. It was proven to be true by a physical exam that had been performed on the young child. This was by far the worst conversation that I had to be involved in, although I like to think that I have tough skin to handle anything.

I applaud anyone who writes about their personal life. I'm actually an introvert who has to force myself to have an extroverted lifestyle because of the type of work that I do, which involves helping others. I can't help others by being quiet. I can't show people that they can make it through adversity if I remain quiet. I wouldn't be able to help my nieces and nephews or the younger generations in my family if I remain quiet. I don't want people to tell my story. I want to tell my own story. I want to leave my mark. I don't want to force anyone to do it for me. And what's the saying…"All that glitters ain't gold"? That is very true.

I am not a perfect person. I'm very flawed. But even through the flaws, there's a beautiful person behind it all. Whenever someone would ask me about the book or what it was about, I would just explain that it was intimate and personal. The process has been somewhat overwhelming. I didn't realize how much time had to be invested in writing a book. It took me about eight months to write the book during my down time; I was told that it would take me two to four years.

I had to tap into moments of my life mentally that weren't so pretty. It drained me on occasion. I would just pace myself during the emotional times. I told myself that it was okay if tears began to fall as I wrote. I kept it in my mind who the book was actually for. Even though this book is made up of snippets of my life and life lessons, it is still for the purpose of reaching others just as much as it has been a process for myself. It was self-healing for me to write. I'm hoping that my writing will be healing for others as well. It was tough reopening up chamber doors of my life. You have to mentally walk down those same paths. Looking back, I don't know how I survived it all. I'm sure that it was the focus of my family that helped me get through. I primarily kept thinking how I needed to take care of my siblings, who I consider my babies, and their babies. For the most part, I see it as emotional control. As long as I can control my composure in most situations, I am able to conquer almost everything.

When I was much younger, I used to hear people mention having out-of-body experiences. I can say that I've had a few of them in my lifetime. Even with me writing this book, I had to mentally step out of myself for moments at a time. I had to mentally and emotionally take myself into a time zone. I had to put myself in a time warp. Even with putting myself in those mental places, I could remember certain smells. I remembered how certain houses smelled or even certain fragrances worn by the people in those instances. It made me realize that there were times of my life that I blocked out and others that I was not able to block out. I know that I'm a much more forgiving person than most people. I'm thankful that I don't have hatred towards certain individuals. I'm thankful that there are still spaces in me where I'm able to let love in. The spaces are not as high or as wide as I'd like them to be, but they are still there. I still love to love. I like that most about myself—that I still love to love on people. I am a goddess. I am a conqueror. I'm a warrior. I see myself as royal. I am one of a kind. I am an originator. I am a leader. I am deep. I am full of wisdom. I am strong. I am revolutionary. I am a mirror to a lot of people. Some of my readers will be able to relate to some of the things I've been faced with while traveling this life's journey.

The more that I write, the lighter I feel. The more that I write, the clearer my mind feels. The more that I write, the clearer my skin becomes. As I write, I am filtering myself. I'm able to filter out the pain, the stress, the burdens, the bondage (no longer a hostage to myself). My heart feels lighter. I'm now lifted. There's much more laughter inside of me ready to come out. I am looking forward to my golden years. The "light switch" has moved to an upward position. Paradise lives within me. I'm able to reach higher within myself. My love is everlasting. I am breathtaking. I am memorable. I am mesmerizing. I am destiny. I am able to receive love again. I am all four seasons. I am light. I am a noble woman. I am a rescuer. I am able to change the heart of others. I am wanted. I am pleasing. I am mind, body, and soul. I am sunshine and rain. I am me.

I come from a generation where it is a common thing to be a high school dropout. I come from a generation of multiple teen births. I was told that I was too boy crazy to further my education. I ended up having six years of college education experience and received a Bachelor's degree and a certification. I want to show my family, friends, and others that when you're faced with adversity, you can grow and become whatever and whomever you want to be. In life, you have to go through those harsh, sticky, mind-altering, and sometimes almost unbearable, moments. At times, in order to go through something, you just have to do simply that—go through it. To get over something is to simply get over it. I know it's easier to say it, but there is positivity after your storms.

"Whatever your hurdles are, continue to smile through it all. Those smiles are part of your mental, physical, and emotional help. Help yourself and continue to smile."
– Toni Rain

"Worry about loving yourself, instead of loving the idea of other people loving you"
– Author Unknown

"Difficult roads often lead to beautiful destinations"
– Author Unknown

"There is no royal road to anything. One thing at a time, all things in succession. That which grows fast withers as rapidly. That which grows slowly, endures"
– Author Unknown

Meeting My Father for the First Time

I had to be about six years old at the time. We were living in an apartment; I hated that apartment. I would even call it embarrassing to live there. It was infested with roaches and mice. I remember having to pick through my Sugar Smacks cereal just to reassure myself that I wasn't eating one of those roaches because to me they looked identical to the cereal that I was eating. One evening, I heard my momma talking to this man that I didn't recognize in my living room. As I walked into the living room, I did a review of this man that I had never seen before. I didn't recognize his features or his voice. My momma was sitting in one chair and this estranged man was sitting on another. "This is your father. I want you to meet him," my mom said to me. It was almost like she was speaking a foreign language to me. I had heard of a father before: I knew that my momma had a father, because I had lived in the same house as her father for almost five years; I was familiar with the term, I just wasn't familiar with it for myself. The room was dark, but I was still able to see his features from the light that was coming from the hallway, as it beamed through the entryway from our front door. This man, my "father", asked me to come to him. He had a smile on his face. My facial expression was blank. I was hesitant. My mom giggled and said, "Go to him. Quit actin' scared girl." But I was scared. No, I was terrified inside. Even as a child, I always tried to be the tough one and try to hide my emotions.

"Know your history"

Fast forward to 13 years later… Again, I was working at a local deli my sophomore year of college. It was a typical day. I was working the deli counter helping customers. While at the counter, I had to slice different meats and cheeses, as well as package different salad items. This day seemed to move at a nice pace. Most of the customers were patient and friendly. There was this one particular individual who walked up to the counter. He looked at the different meat choices. As he glanced around, he just so happened to catch my eye. He was frozen. I asked him if there was anything that I could help him with. He still stood frozen. Eventually, he opened his mouth and the exact words that came out of his mouth were, "You don't know who I am do you?" I was puzzled and had not a clue who this man was. I looked at all of what I could see of him with the deli counter in between the two of us. It still didn't hit me. He inquired about my mother by name. Once I confirmed that she was indeed my mother, he then smiled and said, "You still don't know who I am?"

"Sorry, but no, I do not," I smiled back and replied.

By now I had an uncomfortable grin on my face, as he announced, "Well... I'm your father." Mind you, there were other co-workers around during this exchange.

"Oh wow, I had no idea."

I was even more uncomfortable and very confused. I did not know if I should be happy or sad. I was just about to hit my 20s and I had no familiarity with the man who was known to be my "father". I didn't know whether to jump for joy or yell at the top of my lungs and ask why he hadn't been there for me all those years. I was in a mental turmoil. I don't remember everything that was said after the initial introduction, but I do remember that we exchanged phone numbers to stay in contact with one another. After our conversation, I had to walk to the back area where the cooler was. I could see the air of the frost from the food items swirling all around me. I kept my head held down taking in deep long breaths. Once I felt my body starting to shiver, I snapped out of my mental trance and proceeded to go to the customer counter area. I had to put on a fake smile and conduct myself in an ordinary fashion while there was this mysterious torturing going on inside of my head. From that day forward, things "seemed" like they would get better for me.

"Don't talk, just act. Don't say, just show.
Don't promise, just prove."
–Author Unknown

Experiencing Someone Getting Physically Beaten for the First Time

As I looked down at my bare feet, I could see the light dust on the wooden planks of our floor beneath me. I was stood listening with my ears and listening with my mind. I could hear yells and screams from the apartment beneath me. I had to be around six years old. I was trying to remain calm and still so that I could hear what was going on. My family members were in their bedrooms, as I stood in the living room.

The afternoon sun was shining through the peaks of the curtains. I could hear feet racing back and forth in the apartment below me. I knew the family in the apartment below us. I knew them very well. I wanted to help. Should I help? How could a child of my age help? Should I call the police? How could I even call the police...we didn't even have a telephone. Why was my family not trying to help? Did they hear what I heard? Were they ignoring the screams and yelling? Did they not hear that there were objects being thrown in the apartment below us? Should I yell out the window and call for the police? I didn't know. I didn't know what to do. Moments after I heard the screams, I heard the downstairs door of the apartment slam. After the slam, I heard footsteps pounding on the wooden stairs. Then I heard a loud banging on our door.

Should I open it? I said to myself. I then heard my momma come from the back of our apartment. "Who is it?" she asked. I thought to myself that my momma knew exactly who was at the door. They responded on the opposite end of the door. My momma opened the door and in dashed a lady. She was crying hysterically and dashed to the other side of our apartment. She kneeled down wearing a maternity night gown. As she kneeled, I could see her huge round belly. My mother ran over to comfort her, rubbing her back and telling her that it was going to be okay. Moments later, a man dashed through our apartment door yelling, "Ain't nothin wrong with her, she's alright. Now get your ass back downstairs! There's nothing wrong with you!"

I was frightened but I didn't cry. I just stared at each person in that living room. What was I to do?

> *"If he's a wolf dressed up as a sheep,*
> *his whiskers will inevitably pop out"*
> *–Sherry Argov*

Life Just Is

The man made her run up and down the stairs numerous times naked. I was sitting on a fluffy black sofa, unwrapping one of my favorite pieces of caramel candies. It had a clear wrapper with a red stripe designed on the wrapper. I was swinging my feet forward and backward, hitting the heels of my feet on the sofa. I was either four or five years old. I looked up and I saw her running up and down the stairs. As she ran up and down the stairs, I could tell that she was running out of breath. She slowed down her pace and said, "I can't run anymore, I'm tired." She was naked from head to toe. My eyes no longer focused on the candy. I stopped chewing. I wanted to cry, but I didn't want my sorrows to distract me. My focus was on her now.

I looked to my left and I saw her. I looked to my right and I saw him standing by the entrance door. He yelled at her, "Keep running!!"

"I'm tired." She then picked up her speed then proceeded to keep running back and forth up the stairs. He eventually got distracted and took his focus off of her. She noticed it. I noticed her noticing him lose his focus. She took one more run up the stairs, then on her way back down, she dashed down the stairs and straight out the door. She yelled franticly, "Help me! Somebody please help me! He's trying to kill me! The kids are inside… he's trying to kill me!"

I ran outside behind her. One of the neighbors saw her and ran in their house to grab a sheet. The neighbors grabbed a sheet and wrapped it around her. She sobbed with deep tears running down her eyes. She was looking down. I saw the look of hurt, sadness, and tiredness all over her face. She looked unsure of what to do next or of what she just experienced. She is slumped down and gazed into the cement ground below her. I heard another neighbor say that they were going to call the police. They arrived there within minutes after being called. I remembered being taken to someone's house. Once I arrived at the other house, I was asked so many questions. They asked me if I was okay. One of them said to the other, "I can't believe she's not crying after what just happened, I hope that she's okay." In that moment, I couldn't cry. I was in shock. I didn't know what to think or how to feel. I was a child who watched someone be forced to run up and down a set of stairs multiple times… naked. Why were they making her run? Why did she have sadness in her eyes while doing this? Why didn't she just stop running? Why did she run outside without any clothes on? Why did the neighbors have to call the police? Why did we have to go to someone else's house? Will we have to stay at the other house? Will the police come back to get us? Will we be in trouble? All of these things ran through my head at this gentle age.

"Life is not fair. Life is not unfair. Life just is."
- Eric Jerome Dickey

Seeing Crack and Cocaine for the First Time

One of my cousins and I were taking a walk around the neighborhood. She asked if I could stop by her place for a moment. As we got closer to the house and proceeded to walk to the door, we could hear a lot of commotion from inside. The entrance was connected to the kitchen. When we made it to the door, we could hear and see people standing around an island inside the kitchen. Most of their eyes were bloodshot red. They were loud and playfully yelling at each other. One of them was my aunt. It looked as if they were having a party of some sort. I didn't recall it being my aunt or uncle's birthday party. I didn't see any balloons, food, or cake anywhere in sight, so I wondered what they were celebrating.

I did see alcohol and a bunch of white flour-looking stuff all over the counter. I also saw little glass pipes spread all over the counter, as well as lighters and spoons. They were literally in a "zone". They were oblivious to the fact that we were even around, or perhaps, they didn't even care if we were around. I could recall my uncle laughing and jokingly cursing someone out from one of the other rooms. While he was joking around, I could hear his voice coming closer to us. As he got closer to the kitchen, he and I made eye contact. He yelled to my cousin and I, "Y'all get out of there! You don't need to be in here. I didn't even hear you two come in here. You both need to go to her room."

As my cousin and I were walking to her room, she had a sad look upon her face. I asked her what was wrong and she replied, "Nothing." I insisted that there was something wrong until she finally said, "I'm so tired of them doing that."

"Doing what??"

"You know what they were doing... drugs."

I then explained to her that I didn't know what drugs looked like. I had heard of drugs and had known that people actually did them, but I didn't know what they looked like. I then asked her if her mom and my uncle where doing the drugs also.

"Well... I don't think that he does them, but I know that she does them because I've seen her do them."

*"If you want to fly,
give up everything that weighs you down."*
– Toni Morrison

Seeing Someone Smoke Crack Cocaine for the First Time

My mother was having a "set", which was a term that she and her family and friends used for having a party. Most of these sets would start around 9 or 10 pm. (after my brothers and I were sent to bed). The music would be extremely loud and the apartment would have the aroma of delicious food. My mom was popularly known around the neighborhood for being a wonderful cook, so whenever she was having a gathering, people would definitely show up for the food. I, too, would stay up after we were sent to bed. I knew that if I stayed up long enough and continued to peek my head out the bedroom door from time to time, someone would see me and tell my mom that I was up. I would say to her, "Momma, I can't sleep. It's too loud and my stomach is growling because I'm sooooo hungry." It never failed. She would reply, "Your butt is supposed to be in the bed, but hold on while I make you a plate. You better go right to sleep after you eat it too."

Shortly after she brought me my plate of food and something to drink, I ended up having to use the bathroom. I opened the door of the bedroom and proceeded to go into the hallway. I could hear people partying downstairs. I proceeded to walk to the bathroom. I knocked on the door, but no one responded. I then jerked the door handle to open the door. It felt like someone was either holding the door knob on the opposite side of the door or either leaning their back against the door. I jerked and jerked the door some more until someone let me in. There was a group of about five people compiled in the small compact bathroom. What they were doing in there was not something that was familiar to me. Their words were slurred and their eyes looked as if they were excited. The white of their eyes were red and their eyes were widely opened. One of them asked me, "Baby girl, what are you doing up so late?" I told them that I couldn't sleep and that I needed to use the bathroom. A few of them proceeded to keep their conversation going amongst themselves while holding that glass pipe that I remember seeing at my cousin's house. I knew exactly what they were doing. They were smoking crack cocaine.

They acted as if I wasn't even in their presence. From what I hear, it's a drug that alters your perception of life. I hear that it makes people feel care free, which is probably the reason why some of them proceeded to smoke in my presence. I asked them if it was okay for me to use the toilet because I wasn't able to hold it anymore. They all shuffled out. As I sat there in the bathroom, I could hear them continuing to talk and laugh amongst themselves. My mental light had dimmed. I was trying to figure out how they could be filled with laughter and smiles while doing something that I was told was a "bad" thing. I was questioning myself: *Does my mom know what they were doing in here? Will I be punished for seeing them smoke that stuff? Will they tell on me that I saw them? Should I tell my momma what they were doing? Should I wake my brothers to tell them what I had just seen? Will my momma go to jail because they are doing drugs in our house? I don't want my momma to go to jail. If my momma goes to jail, who will keep me and my brothers? Will we have to live at grandma and grandpa's house if momma goes to jail?* I was so confused. I didn't know what to do or think.

"We don't meet people by accident.
They are meant to cross our path for a reason"
– Author Unknown

He Said That He Was Listening for Trains Outside My Bedroom Window

We stayed in a two-level apartment. My bedroom was in the far corner of the apartment. There was a railroad track near our residence. So many nights I would awake to the vibrations of the train causing our windows to shake. The sounds of the train's horn would often wake me up out of my sleep. Other times, I would awake to my little brothers coming into my room because they couldn't sleep. One night was so different.

I was asleep in an almost pitch-dark room. The only light that was coming through my window was from the moon's light. I could hear the voice of someone whom sounded familiar. I could hear them repeatedly calling my name. At first, I thought that I was dreaming, when, in fact, I was not. I opened my eyes to see who was there hovering over me. I noticed the outline of the face. I then heard her say, "Did he touch you? Do not lie. Did he touch you?"

"Did who touch me?" I asked.

"I didn't touch her, I was looking out of the window listening for the train," said another voice that I recognized. After that, the two of them began to argue. I was so confused. I was half asleep and didn't really know what was going on. Once I came to my senses, I knew exactly what could've happened. He was not really listening for trains. He was listening and watching me.

"Look for something positive in each day, even if some days you have to look a little harder"
- From inspirationalquotesmagazine.com

A Continuous Act of Incest

There is a relative who loved to be around me to say the least. I was in elementary school. He was some years older. He would always ask his mom if I was going to be able to stay the night at their house. Even though his mom was supposed to be keeping her eyes on us, she rarely did. He would always want me to watch movies with him. He would get so excited and animated about me being able to come over. The movies wouldn't even be on for more than 10 minutes before he decided to make a move on me. There was no intercourse involved (thankfully). There was kissing and what the kids would call "humping". For some reason he would always want to "hump" me. Internally, I knew that what he was doing wasn't appropriate.

I would just lay there, petrified, and let him do that to me. I didn't know if or who I should even tell. I didn't know if I would get in trouble for telling. I didn't want to be bullied or harassed. I didn't want his mom to be upset with me. I didn't want my mom to be upset with me. I just didn't want anyone to be upset.

"Just because I laugh a lot doesn't mean my life is easy. Just because I have a smile on my face doesn't mean something isn't bothering me. I just chose not to dwell on negative things and move on with my life."
– Author Unknown

Changing My Views
When It Comes to Religion

When it comes to religion, most of my memories are with my family. Most of my experience as a child was going to a Pentecostal Christian church with my grandmother and other family members. I remember most of the women wearing skirts that went to their ankles and wearing very little to no makeup. The women in our family looked much different from most of the women of the church. I say that, because most of the women in my family did wear makeup or, at the least, wore lipstick.

In my mind, I knew that my family stuck out. I would see the faces of the other families of the church snarled sometimes when we would come through those church doors. I also noticed that we were the only family that liked to wear pretty decorative pantyhose (some of them lace) with our dresses. My family actually refer to pantyhose as "stockings". I'm guessing that some of the people of the church didn't approve of that either. I remember having a conversation with one of the little girls of the church, them grilling me with questions as to why me and the other ladies in my family wore fancy stockings. The little girl told me that I dressed too "fast". A girl who was labeled "fast" was looked at as being too adult-like for her age. In my eyes, the decorative stockings were what I was used to seeing. In fact, I thought they were very fun and pretty to wear. I liked the fact that our style of dress stood out. We were known as the family who stuck out most of my life anyway. I also liked to wear perfume to church and some of the other girls used to make smart comments about that as well. Some of their families didn't think it was appropriate for little girls to wear perfume either.

Other members of my family grew up in Baptist and Episcopal churches. I remember some of my family who attended the other churches telling me and other family members that we didn't dress appropriately for church. I felt as if we were shunned when it came to attending church. I've heard all my life that you are to "come as you are" in regards to attending church. Was this statement actually true?! I often questioned if it was.

One day after school, our family had a few visitors from the Church of Jesus Christ of Latter-day Saints come to our house. They asked if they could talk to me and my family for a few hours. My mom invited them in to see what they had to say. It was the first time any church members wanted to spend quality time with our family, so we welcomed them with open arms. They even offered to give us rides from our house to their church since we did not have the transportation. We looked at this as another nice and welcoming gesture. We ended up joining the church.

It was much different from the other churches that we attended. I was always used to praise and worship services, whereas this church didn't really have that same type of feel. Another thing that stood out to me was the lack of diversity in the church. Most of the churches that I attended were diverse with different ethnic groups. This caused me to raise an eyebrow. I was also surprised to learn that I was able to baptize my family members and they were able to baptize me. It was interesting to know that the Church of Jesus Christ of Latter-day Saints was considered the Mormon church and they even had a Mormon book that they lived by.

I remember members of my family and friends frowning upon the fact that my family had joined a Mormon church. I'm the type of person that likes to find my way and navigate through life on my own terms. I want to find out the truth on my own of what's right and not right for me. I want to learn where I fit in when it comes to life. I don't want, or allow, others to make decisions for me. Once I did learn more about the Mormon church, I found that it wasn't a good fit for me either. I didn't agree with a lot of their teachings. Most of the Mormon members that I came in contact looked down on other members of society if they were not members of their church. Because I didn't feel comfortable attending any of those churches, I decided to try a non-denominational church, where I did feel much more comfortable. There was versatility in the way that people dressed and in personalities. I liked the fact that the choirs were into their music. I have a passion for most genres of music.

There were a few life altering situations that I was dealing with too. Since childhood I had been told to "take your problems to the church". It was exactly what I did. I took some personal things that I was going through to the church. Instead of taking my problems to the alter, I took them to some of the head people of the church. Not even 30 minutes after I had this personal conversation with those few members of the church, that same information came right back to me. That was the last straw for me. I knew in that moment that I would not be back to that church or any other church as far as membership was concerned. The only other times that I have been back to church were for funeral services.

Unfortunately, I've met some of the most ill-willed wicked people at church or those who claim to be people of the church. I've personally found that most don't "practice what they preach" either. Many of the men who are of the church are the ones who like to step out on their women and have tried to "entertain" me. I've also been told that they would like to "lay hands" on me and not in a way that would be appropriate for "the church". From my own experience, I've found that many people who focus their lives on religion are hypocritical. I try to live my truth as much as possible, so it's hard for me to be around people who are not authentic or genuine. Own your truth. Even if your truth may not be considered as righteous or correct in the eyes of others, still own it. Otherwise, it can eat you up emotionally. Trust me… I've been there in my younger years to know this.

I've also noticed that many people who live religious lifestyles do the complete opposite of the lifestyle they're supposed to live by. Judgment is the #1 thing that is contradicted. I've been judged the most by people of "the church". I have friends who are avid church attenders. I still love them. I believe that if you live a positive and loving life, then you will get far in life. I believe that if you put good into the world, then the world will continue to put good into you. Regardless of the things that have happened to me that were considered as bad, I still put out good energy. I know that life is not going to be all bad. Circumstances that aren't within my control are going to happen. Thankfully, I can say that more good has happened than bad. I believe in a universal love, not a religious love. Religion is another form of segregation and hate towards humankind in my eyes. I still believe that there is a Creator (God) who embraces us without having to join any religious groups.

"Be yourself no matter what other people think. God made you the way you are for a reason. Besides, an original is always worth more than a copy."
- Author Unknown

The Sacrificial Lamb

I have always seen myself as a "sacrificial lamb". I told my brothers to use my personal situations as an example of how not to treat the women in their lives. I remember standing in the kitchen talking to my brothers about a particular milestone that I was going through. I told them, "You see... just how you don't want a man putting their hands on your mother or your sister, no one wants you guys to put your hands on their mother or their sisters either. I want you guys to see me as an example of hurt and pain. You see how men have caused hurt and pain in my life. I don't want you to put that same type of hurt in someone else's life. You see firsthand what it looks like and how it can affect someone."

I have only shared a small piece of my life story. Some of the things that I've been faced with would probably be too heavy for my readers. I see myself as a "sacrificial lamb" by the Creator. I feel that I am used as an example of being able to take the world by storm. The "winds" of the world have tried to blow me down, but I ALWAYS get back up. I have been on battlefields that most women wouldn't be able to survive. I learned as a child that no matter what struggles I go through, I still keep up my womanhood. By keeping my womanhood, I have to make sure that I look presentable in the public eye. I always make sure that I'm well-groomed and clean. Even those days I don't feel like getting dressed for the day, I always make sure that I do anyways. They say, "If you stay ready, then you don't have to get ready." I figured if I am always presentable and ready for success, then I don't have to get ready for success. You just never know when you may get that call or get asked to come in for that meeting that you've been waiting for. The Creator created me to be strong. The Creator wants others to see my pains and strife and see how a person like me can survive almost anything.

"Your yesterday is not your tomorrow"
- Author Unknown

My Senior Year of High School

One of the hardest years that I had to get through was my senior year of high school. It's the year that most people look forward to. It's the year right before you hit your adulthood. It's the year that you look forward to throwing up your graduation cap and tassels. For most people, it's the year that you get prepared to go off to college. Even with all these things in my thoughts and my mind, I had to face other truths of reality. One of my most life changing events was getting pregnant my senior year of high school. It literally changed my life forever. I don't remember a time when I was most scared than when I became pregnant. I hid it from the world, so I thought. I told a few people, but I refused to tell the one person who I should've told before anyone else...my mother. Quite frankly, most of the ones that I did tell about this private situation shouldn't have been told at all. The messed up part about this pregnancy was that it was terminated. It's certainly not something that I was proud of then, and it's certainly not something that I'm proud of now. I blamed a lot of things that were detrimental in my life on that decision to terminate my pregnancy. I'm a strong believer in karma, so I felt that all the misfortunes I was faced with after the termination was due to me. It was my first and only pregnancy of my life. The twisted part about it is that I actually love children dearly.

During my senior year, I was faced with homelessness—moving from place to place. There was also a time during that year when we did have a place to stay. We had other relatives living with us at that time and they, too, were homeless during my senior year of high school. We also had other hardships that year. We had a drug addict who was living with us whom was constantly lying, stealing, and bringing outsiders in our home. The energy was so negatively heavy and draining. At one point, I didn't know or even think that I was going to make it through. It was so hard hiding and keeping my emotions inside. I felt like I was in a whirlwind...no, I felt like I was in the "Twilight Zone". I felt as if I was going to go mentally crazy. I became so disappointed in myself. I was disappointed in the father of the baby because he lied to me about contraception. I felt like I was going to let down my entire family. I felt like I was going to let the naysayers have control and power of my life if had kept the baby. I didn't want to be a "product of my environment". I was already drained with what I had going on at home. I was an honor roll student from elementary through all of my years of high school. I didn't want to let down my instructors who were cheering for me on the side lines. I wanted to keep all of my friends out of the know of what was going on in my world. I was one of the popular ones and I didn't want to lose my status. In fact, I was voted prom queen. The week of prom, I had to get dressed at a relative's house because of our living situation. I was even on the homecoming court. There was so much irony in that one little year. How can someone juggle highs and lows like that? It was literally enough to make anyone go crazy.

"Life is like an ocean. It can be calm or still, and rough or rigid, but in the end, it is always beautiful."
– Author Unknown

My Male Military Mission

It took for me to look at the souls of my brothers and my grandfather to have respect for men. I pretty much had no respect for men. I saw them as "play things" and that was it. My feelings became numb towards them. Men would oftentimes fall in love with me. I often pretended to fall in love with them, but it was mostly a facade. It was a game. I knew that I was a passionate lover, so I knew that they would be hooked. Once they got hooked, I led them astray. I would throw them away and out of my mind as if they never existed. I would catch them by surprise. I was on a mental mission to destroy them. I wanted to destroy them for hurting me and other women like me. I felt as if I was on a "male military mission." So many of my family members, my family members' friends, and my friends would tell me stories of the BS that they would endure from men. The stories turned me into something nonhumane. I became dull. I became a machine. I saw no real or true feelings in boys and men. They didn't deserve that love that I was longing to give. Only the women deserved that love. Not in a sexual way, but in an "I'm so sorry that society did this to you" kind of way. I even had it set in my mind that I was going to show and teach my nieces and every other young lady or woman that I came in contact with how to manipulate these men. I wanted to protect them. I wanted to protect them from their future hurt, pain, and agony.

Women would sometimes envy me because men would flock down to my feet. Those that were close to me knew the mental game that I was playing. They would get upset with me at times because they didn't have the ability to lure men the way that I did. They would think that my looks were the reason why I was able to pull it off. In fact, my looks had very little to do with it. It was 90% mental. Some of the men that I took advantage of never even knew if I was a woman or a man, meaning they had never seen me without my clothes on. I could pretty much lure a man into doing whatever I wanted him to do without even having sex. I didn't have a lot of respect for married men especially. Most of them would want to approach me and risk their entire livelihood and home just for a moment with me. I felt disgusted. So many times, I wanted to out them. I've outed a few of them, but most times it would backfire on me. The women would get upset with me for their men wanting me. It was a physiological issue with the women I figured. I was taught that when a man steps out on a woman, that the woman should approach the man and not the woman. Only under certain circumstances that you should approach the man and the woman. If the woman is a close friend or relative, then you should approach her as well, because she was aware that the husband/wife or girlfriend/ boyfriend are involved. If she's a complete stranger or oblivious of the situation, then you are to just approach the man. Even if the other party is a stranger or oblivious to the situation, more times than not, they aren't going to care if you are involved, because they have no personal emotions attached to you. Many times, they aren't going to be empathetic to your emotions if there are no personal attachments. You will more than likely be wasting your time trying to tell the other woman or man how they've hurt you by sleeping with their partner or significant other. Better yet, sometimes you will give that other person that satisfaction of thinking that they stole or took something that was very valuable to you from you. Some people get a thrill of thinking that they have corrupted someone else's home. There are a lot of selfish people and some are proud that they are selfish.

I refuse to give people that satisfaction of feeling like they have that much power over me. Allowing someone to have that much power over me would just take me to those times in life where I felt powerless over my living or sexual experiences that I had as a child. It would just take me back to the beginning of my life and I wasn't going to let that flow back into my uncomfortable mental state. I had to look at the love that I had for my brothers and grandfather. The love that I had for them allowed me to learn to have respect for men. Their love towards me and other women in my family showed me that a man can have genuine love inside of them. If they had that love, I was able to see that there could possibly be as much love in other men. I just had to let some guards down to see if it stood true.

"A smart man makes a mistake, learns from it, and never makes that mistake again. But a wise man finds a smart man and learned from him how to avoid the mistake all together." - Roy H. Williams

When a Man Loves a Woman

A man who truly loves a woman, does not make her past his focal point. His focal point becomes her soul. Some people's pasts may be viewed as being darker than others. Even those with dark pasts should be treated with respect. So often I hear the terms: hoe, slut, tramp, thot, or bitch. There are so many different personality types and lifestyles that people live. Some are chosen and some are due to life situations. Either way, I believe in women being treated with respect no matter what type of lifestyle they live. Some of us have grandmothers, mothers, aunts, daughters, sisters, cousins, and nieces that have dark pasts. When it comes to family members, I feel that they are given a pass. Then the moment it's seen from someone not of relation, then they are quickly judged.

I've seen that men/women can be attracted to women/men with dark pasts. In my mind, I figure that they are able to do this because they are able to look past their previous lifestyle because they are able to see the person for who they are and not for the way that they have lived. I like to look for the good in people. I also think that some men look and focus on the soul of women. From my experience with dating and relationships, I was up front with them about how certain things in my life affected me when it came to dealing with men. I let it be known that they would have to put in work when being with me. I was told on many occasions that I had a beautiful soul despite certain things that went on in my life. They were able to look past things that were seen as being dark in my life. I've been disrespected by men of course, but there has been more love poured into me than there has been hurt.

"The deepest principle in human nature
is the craving to be appreciated." - William James

I Tried to Get My Ex to Help Me Sell Drugs...
But He Declined

I grew up with a childhood friend that I eventually started dating. It was more so puppy love. We were very young and focusing on our teenage life. Our bond was strong due to the fact that we were both silly and loving to others. He was known for his bright smile and his upbeat personality. He lived a fast-paced life in the streets. I looked past his street life and loved him for his strong friendship. I noticed that he would wear expensive named brand clothes. I also knew that he was into illegal drugs. During the time, there were family members and friends into the street life, so it was a norm for me seeing things like this. I knew that for some of them, that lifestyle was a part of their survival. Many of them had come from low-income homes and they were just trying to help their families. Most of my life, I tried to live a judge free lifestyle. Everyone has their reasons for doing certain things or living a certain way and it was never my place to try to make them feel less humane than I was.

A few times, my antennas went up in regards to wanting to live that same lifestyle. In my mind, I felt that I wouldn't have as many stresses. I was also thinking about my household. I was tired of seeing my mother and my brothers struggling financially. I was tired of going without necessities. I was tired of seeing my mother having to ask for handouts from other people for us. I was tired of seeing the sadness in my brother's eyes from not being able to fit in at school because they dressed different from some of the other children. I was just tired. Eventually, I tried to slide over to the other lifestyle. I tried to slide over to the "street life". I talked to a relative on how to get started. I even asked how much money I needed to start off with in order for them to want to work for me. Once I talked it over with my relative, I went home to think things through.

One day I was on my front porch and my then-boyfriend came to visit me. I told him that I needed to talk to him about something important. He had this puzzling look on his face the moment I started to talk about it. The puzzling look turned into him being very uncomfortable. I eventually pulled something out of my pocket. He immediately shook his head no. He told me that I was not about that kind of life. He asked me to get rid of it. Even though he was doing the same thing, he didn't want me to have any involvement with it. I tried to explain that I needed money to provide for my family. He explained to me that it wasn't my responsibility to take care of my family and that I was too young to put that burden on myself. After our talk, he kissed my forehead, held me tight, and told me things would get better. He refused to help me with wanting to live that lifestyle. During that time in my life, I didn't realize the risk I was taking because I saw so many people selling drugs and never saw them get caught. I was naive and had no clue how my life could've changed for the worst getting involved. Even the biggest gangsters and drug dealers get caught. So many people lose their lives in the drug world. Innocent lives are also taken. I'm glad that I chose a different lifestyle path.

"There has never been a meaningful life built on easy street" - *John Paul Warren*

Harassment on the Job

It all started prior to this employee being hired for a position in our department. They actually had another job title during my initial encounter with meeting them. Needless to say, I was given a hard time the first time we ever crossed paths. The first time that we met, they were to assist me because it was a part of their job assignment. I was greeted with one of the worse customer service experiences of my life from this person. I even had to ask for their manager to help them with assisting me. Not long after our initial encounter with one another, they ended up applying for a position at the place of employment where I was working. The moment they walked into the area of where I was working on their first day of their new position, we locked eyes with one another. On their end, it was like a deer caught in headlights. Their eyes were wide and bucked the moment they looked at me. I knew that they remembered me. I for sure remembered them as well. From that day, I was hoping that I didn't have to experience the type of attitude and lack of respect that I had experienced from our initial encounter. Sure enough, I experienced the rudeness and more.

Throughout the duration of time that we had to work together, I was constantly being watched. As a matter of fact, I was being cyber stalked outside of work as well. This person requested me as a friend on social media, in which I denied the request. There was talk amongst other employees about how they were stalking my social media pages. My pages were set to "private", but this person still found ways to manipulate that fact. They would set up fake accounts or have others that they know request me as a "friend" or a "follow". I'm guessing that this wasn't enough for them in regards to stalking and harassment. From what I was told by others, they were keeping tabs on when I would take my restroom breaks as well. I felt like I constantly had someone watching my every move.

I kept quiet about it initially. I thought that they would eventually back off. At times, I felt like I was in a cage. I felt like I was constantly under watch and under attack from an energy standpoint. There was a coworker that described the employee that was harassing others as being evil. I had other staff coming to me telling me about how they were being bullied and harassed by this same person as well. This person was finding ways to manipulate others in many ways, in which I won't go into details with due to confidentiality reasons. Most of the staff felt intimidated by this person. I, for sure, was not in fear of them or intimidated by them. I was actually brave enough to confront them on it. I went to higher authority to report some of the incidents of harassment. Of course, this person denied it. If you or anyone that you know is being harassed on your job, be the voice and stand up for yourself. Don't ever let someone else overshadow you or make you feel uncomfortable in your place of employment. You may not just be making the decision to be in a comfortable environment for yourself, but you may also be helping others to work in a safe and comfortable environment. Your voice is more impactful than you think.

"Never be bullied into silence. Never allow yourself to be made a victim. Accept no one's definition of your life; define yourself." - Tim Fields

Bittersweet Sunny Days

So, one day I was trying to pinpoint when I experienced my very first orgasm. I want to say it was about the age of five years old. I was outdoors playing with a group of neighborhood and family children. I remember one of them saying that we are all going to play a game. The name of the game was called "Hide and Go Get It". Now, as a young child at that young age of five, I had no clue as to the way this "game" was played. All I knew is that the older children were all smiles and full of excitement, ready to play. One of the little boys told me to hide, and he was going to go get it. In that moment, I had not a clue what he was going to go get. In my mind I figured it had to be a toy or some candy, perhaps. The girls were all told to hide and the other boys were assigned to "go get it" as well.

I specifically remember where I hid. It was at one of the houses up the street from where my relatives lived. They had a large hill where a cement wall laid on the sides to keep the hill still and steady. I decided to hide alongside the hill against that cement wall, with it serving as my protection in my hiding space. I could hear footsteps. After a few steps, I could hear them pause and then proceed to walk again. Eventually, I was found. I looked up with surprise and a grin on my face. His face had a grin also. His face went from a grin to stone. Once his facial expression changed, mine became a reflection of his. I became silent. I didn't know what to expect, but I knew that what followed was unfamiliar to me. He told me to lay back. Now mind you, I'm a five-year-old child not knowing what was going to happen. We were playing a "game". Without any further words or phrases, this boy, fully dressed, laid his body over mine. I just remember being still and frozen in the moment. I was confused—very confused. As he lay on top of me, I could feel the warmth from the hot summer weather; his clothes rubbing against mine while I stared up at a beautiful picture of nature's sky.

Even at this tender age, I knew this wasn't a game. He knew this wasn't a game. I remember snapping in and out of myself; I was snapping in and out of what was happening to me and what I was seeing with my eyes wide open. What was going on was bittersweet. I think that was where I fell in love with nature. I could see the clouds passing by. I knew that they were called clouds because I had learned about them from my preschool teacher.

"When something bad happens you have three choices. You can either let it define you. Let it destroy you, or you can let it strengthen you."
- Dr. Seuss

They Say Music Heals the Soul

All I kept thinking to myself was, *Momma, please don't leave me.* So many times I had repeated that line inside my head. It seemed as if it was a tune that had played over and over like the same number of times I watched the vinyl spin on the record player at my grandparents' house. I used to adore watching that record spin on the turntable. I adored it because in those moments I knew that I was safe. I was safe from the chaos that was a continuous notion inside of a few homes. Maybe that's where my passion for music comes from. Maybe it has always been my safety net. I actually love music more than I love people at times.

"Sometimes the best thing you can do is not think, not wonder, not imagine, not obsess. Just breathe, and have faith that everything will work out for the best"
- Author Unknown

Seeing Someone Have Sex for the First Time

It was a very sunny Saturday afternoon. The apartment was warm and the temperature felt just right. I was around the age of seven years old. In the area where we lived, there was a train that would pass just behind our backyard. The train was so close to our residence that it caused our entire complex to shake.

There were other relatives visiting that day. I remember one of my female cousins bringing a guy over with her. As usual, I spent most of my days outdoors. I would often times just go back inside just to get something to eat or drink. I'd also have to take occasional bathroom breaks as anybody would. During one of my breaks, I walked across my bedroom. I noticed something that I had never seen or experienced before. I could see the top of a man's legs intermingled with the legs of someone else on top of his. I stood in silence because I didn't know what else to do. I didn't know if I should say something, keep watching, or turn around as if I saw nothing. I didn't know if what I was seeing was wrong or if me seeing what was going on would cause me to be punished.

As I saw the overlapping legs, I started to glance at the rest of their bodies. They were both fully naked, but the guy still had on his socks. My cousin was moving in a slow upward and downward motion. She had her eyes closed, so she didn't even notice that I was watching. Her guy friend had a tight grip holding the sides of her waist. He was groaning, which from a child's standpoint I thought that he was in pain. In my mind I asked myself the following questions: *What are they doing? What is going on? Does it hurt? Is she trying to hurt him? Why is he letting her hurt him like that?! Should I go tell my momma what they are doing? Should I tell my momma that my cousin is hurting her friend and he's just lying there letting her do that to him? Why are her eyes closed...what is she doing?? Why don't they have on any clothes? Why are they in my bed? Who told them that they could come in MY room and get into my bed?*

After standing and observing them for a short while, I decided to go into the living room. I could feel the look of confusion on my face. I didn't know what to do or what to say. I ended up talking briefly to one of my aunts, trying to explain what I had seen. I always felt free to talk to her about almost everything. I think it had something to do with her age. She was much younger than my mother, so I felt that she would be relatable to the situation since her and my cousin were closer in age. I didn't feel comfortable going to my mother about it. Deep down inside, I felt that me knowing what had just happened was something that I shouldn't know about or had even seen. Even though it was accidental, I still felt that I was at fault for walking into the situation—a situation that I wasn't even familiar with.

While talking to my aunt, I said, "I saw hair 'down there'. I didn't know that boys had hair down there." The look on my aunt's face was priceless. She was in shock and she looked uncomfortable. There was even an uncomfortable burst of laughter from her to go along with her look. Later that day, my mom pulled me to the side and asked why had I watched my cousin and her friend. I told her that I was coming from the bathroom and noticed that someone was in my bedroom. She had a shameful smirk on her face and said okay but then proceeded to say, "You shouldn't be talking about boys having 'hair down there either."

"Keep your face to the sunshine and you cannot see a shadow"
– Helen Keller

My Brothers Physically/Mentally Fighting My Mother's Battles

I grew up in a single-parent household throughout my entire life, up until I moved out at the age of 18. Most of my life, people would tell me that I never really acted like a child. They would say that I "thought I was grown". I didn't really fit in with anyone my age. Whenever people were around, I most often would gravitate to the adults. One thing that I noticed about being in a single-parent household, was that my momma would often date. I guess you could say that she was always looking for love. Love always seemed to be looking for her too. I sometimes used to wonder if she was just looking for love for her or was she looking for love for all of my siblings and myself.

A few of them would buy groceries for our entire family or purchased food from local restaurants. When they would come around, they would always appear as charming. I remember some of them would ask my mom questions like, "What's wrong with her??" "She looks so mean!" They were referring to me. I was known for having a mean and serious expression on my face. It was my way of guarding and protecting my family whenever someone new would come around. I was always guarded and I'm still guarded to this day actually. I seem to have this "no bullshit" persona about myself, and I've never been ashamed to admit that. Now, my brothers, on the other hand, they were the complete opposite of me. Instead of them guarding themselves with their facial expressions, they would guard themselves with their words. If there was a situation that would arise between my mother and her boyfriends and/or partners that wasn't approved by my brothers, they had no problem voicing how they felt. Sometimes things would get physical. Some of my brothers had tempers.

When things would get out of hand and problems escalated, my brothers would step in. Their small bodies would not be able to stop a grown man from being physical with a woman, but they didn't seem to care about that. If a battle was fought between my mother and her guys, my brothers would jump in to help her. Me, on the other hand, I never did try to help physically fight her battles. I would go in shut-down mode. I would mentally try to escape the yelling, fighting, and throwing of objects. My eyes would stay on the reoccurring situations, but my voice would go silent. My limbs would feel weakened. I wouldn't be able to throw a physical blow with my fists even if I wanted to. I knew that if I was to challenge a grown man in a physical fight as a child, that I would lose. I would lose just like she did. I had seen it happen too many times.

It was a repeated cycle. She would find a new lover. Things would always look good in the beginning. They'd get mentally, emotionally, or physically abusive with my mom. My brothers would jump in to help her fight her battles. I'd go into shut-down mode. Her lovers would leave. The cycle would then repeat.

"Fight back with your mind, not with your heart."
– A Woman's Guidebook Through Heartache

Fighting My Battles

I used physical, verbal, and emotional abuse to fight my battles; using violence as a way of coping with my childhood stress and pain (literally fighting my battles). From as far as I could remember, I was always a physical fighter. I remember fighting classmates, neighborhood friends, and family members if I felt threatened or disrespected. Since a child, boxing has always been my favorite sport. I love to watch it and I like boxing as a form of exercise. I also didn't take lightly to anyone cornering or showing disrespect to my siblings. I felt like a momma bear protecting her cubs when it came to my siblings. I've always felt like their shelter and their comfort. It's still that way. I'm very over protective of them. Most people figure that out once they meet us.

Growing up, I've always had a temper, a smart mouth, and was always ready to fight when I felt or saw disrespect. I didn't take lightly to school bullies either. I didn't recognize it until I got older that I brought a lot of my childhood anger and frustration with me into my adult years. I found myself letting my frustrations out physically because that's what I grew up seeing. I didn't just see it in my home, but in the homes of other relatives and friends' homes as well. I thought it was the thing to do. In fact, I thought that all families fought in this manner. I pretty much fought each year that I was in elementary school. One time I even pulled my brothers out of school (as if I was their parent), because they told me that they were being bullied by other classmates. The principal tried to stop me from taking my brothers out of school, but I cursed her out and told her that I could do what I wanted to do. I was only in the fifth grade at that time.

Looking back, I could see that it wasn't a smart decision. I should've let my momma handle it. In that moment, I felt like an adult and thought that I was doing the right thing by trying to protect my siblings. A few times, I had fought groups of girls by myself. Once I fought a group of girls on a public school bus. Looking back, I was insane for doing that. Even with all of the physical violence that was going on, I still remained an honor student throughout my adolescent years. No matter what I was going through, my education always remained a priority. I even looked at my education as a battle field. Most of my family either dropped out of middle school or high school. Quitting school was never even a thought. I looked at education as a means for getting out of that hostile environment, not even considering that my anger would move into my adulthood as well.

Most of my frustrations were locked in my mental. I was not big into studying while I was in school. I didn't feel that I had to study since things stuck with me naturally. Most times, I would study either the day or the morning before a test. Ironically, I looked at my focus on what I needed for a test as a battlefield as well. I was taking on a task head to head. Me taking a quiz or an exam was me fighting my way through another victorious win. I was winning against the naysayers who tried to fill my head into thinking that I was going to give up just like most of the people in my family had done. Failure or losing was not an option for me.

"Life is 10% what happens to us and 90% how we react to it."
– Dennis P. Kimbro

Using Sex as a Means to Cope with My Pain

I remember my first time having intercourse. It was so cold outside. I literally trekked my way through the snow to get to my boyfriend at the time. I was feeling all of these different emotions. I had already known what an orgasm felt like. In fact, I was addicted to orgasms. I just hadn't experienced having sexual intercourse.

There were so many lies being exchanged that day in order for us to make it happen. We didn't care. We had one thing on our mental and that was getting to our "business". I still remember the music video that was playing on his TV when I walked into his room. I think that I was more ready to get to it than he was. He seemed so nervous. He knew that it was my first time, but it wasn't his first time. Me being the competitive, spirited person that I am, I decided to "ride" my first time. I had no idea what I was in for. It was very painful once we were finished. I tried to act as if it was something easy to handle.

After the act, all I could think about was when I would be able to do it again. In just a short period of time, I became addicted. I actually became a sex addict. It became my drug. I wanted it almost every day. Sex seemed to put me in a galaxy, especially cunnilingus. With all the stresses and living conditions that I was in, sex seemed to be my #1 outlet. After I reached my peak, it seemed like everything that was causing me to feel down disappeared for that moment. My drive seemed to be higher than the guys that I dated, so I was never full or satisfied.

I was never into drugs or alcohol. I actually didn't start drinking casually until after I graduated college. Prior, I had tried a few drinks, but I didn't really like alcohol. The only high that I wanted came from sex. I chased that natural high. I was warned not to abuse it, but this life lesson didn't seem to stick with me. It took for me to be outed by "friends" to get my addiction under control. I've actually spoken to someone professionally about it. I've learned ways of channeling that energy into other areas of my life. I've learned how to suppress those feelings. Sex can be just as addicting as any drug. It takes strength to admit that sex addiction is present and it takes strength to want to get help for it.

"We are human. We are not perfect. We are alive. We try things. We make mistakes. We stumble. We fall. We get hurt. We rise again. We try again. We keep learning. We keep growing. And...we are thankful for the priceless opportunity called life."
- From lovethispic.com

Using Food as a Way to Cope with My Pain

Weight loss and gain has always been a part of me. I was the largest child in my household. The irony of it is that on several occasions I've had major weight loss throughout my life. When I would gain a lot of weight, people would comment on it. When I would lose a lot of weight, people would comment on it. Most of the whispers and comments came from family. Very few of the comments came from friends. In all honesty, family will cut and tear you down with words quicker than anyone on the streets.

Everyone has their addictions. One of my addictions just so happens to be food. I was never into drugs and alcohol. I started drinking, wine primarily, socially after I finished college. I knew the effects that drugs and alcohol had on someone, so that wasn't something that I wanted to alter my life. Food was always part of my life. Most of the adults in my family cooked all the time. My mother is an amazing cook, so food was always around. In my household, I ate more than everyone. I was also the one to sample the meals or new recipes that my mom would make. Sampling the food was one of my favorite things to do. Simply put, food made me happy. I loved the taste and the smell of food. It would light up my senses as well as my taste buds.

As an adult, I learned that some foods are aphrodisiacs. Some foods actually can arouse a person. Food did that to me as well. Some foods actually gave me a sexual appetite...especially spicy foods. I always had a craving for spicy foods. I've never really been a fan of the sweeter foods. The sweets didn't really do it for me. I also ate more when I was stressed. The more stressed I got, the more I ate. Once I realized that my weight would go up drastically, I would get stressed even more. To cover up that stress, I would eat even more to try to make myself feel whole again. It was a repeated cycle. I was covering up more and more pain, so I was gaining more and more weight.

I was fighting against myself with food. It took me many years to realize what I was doing. It took for me to look at pictures to see what I was doing to myself. It's crazy how you can look in the mirror and see yourself every day and not notice drastic changes with your body, but, instead, it takes for someone else to notice the changes in your body and appetite. When you are "covering up" with food, sometimes that's all you see is the food. Sometimes you don't recognize yourself and the world around you. All you see is what's on your plate and what you want to see on your plate.

More than anything, I was consuming more of the wrong types of food. I was more interested in the unhealthy foods, particularly greasy foods. I knew that I had to get my eating habits under control because I didn't want to start having health issues. I didn't want to clog up my arteries or play with my heart. I had to make a change. I still love to eat. I just learned to love foods that were actually good for me as well as foods that were good to me. I always loved fruits and vegetables. My husband introduced me to "green juicing". We received a juicer as a gift. It sat around for a while. My husband started to use it and try different recipes. As a result, I learned that vegetables have a low-calorie count. In fact, a lot of people do not even count the calories of vegetables because the count is so low. I knew I could eat as many vegetables as I wanted without the guilt. So, I made juicing a new part of my lifestyle. If I got stressed, it didn't bother me that I drank a full cup of vegetable juice. I was able to do my body a service of making it feel better again by healing it with vitamins and nutrients. The key was using my passion for eating but using it in a more positive manner. I had to realize that eating wasn't so bad after all. It was all in the way of how it was done. Even with my major weight losses and gains, they didn't keep me from getting attention. I was told that no matter how much I weighed, I'd always have a beautiful heart and face. Them saying that made me realize that I had more to offer than just my body.

"The journey of a thousand miles begins with one step." - Lao Tzu

Living Life Backwards as a Child-like Adult

I was often told that I was "grown" as a child. I was told that I never really acted my age. I'll admit that I was very mature for my age growing up. Partially, it was because I had to grow up fast. I was the eldest child in my household so I had a lot of responsibilities. I knew at a tender age that my mother needed help. Even as a child, my adult-like instincts kicked in early. I caught on to things early as well. If I watched my mother do something, I was able to pick it up and mimic what she would do.

I saw my mother struggling. Always being an empathetic person, I wasn't going to watch her do it alone. I saw the hurt and struggle in her eyes and in her emotions. If I was able to help, that was exactly what I was going to do. I was sorting clothes by colors and washing clothes by hand at the age of four (I'm also talking about washing jeans by hand...that wasn't easy to do). I knew how to clean an entire kitchen by the age of five. I knew how to cook some food items by the age of five. I also developed physically at a young age. I was wearing a D-cup size in bras by the time I graduated from elementary school. I was known as the "kid with the big breasts". I used to hate walking around the neighborhood. I felt like a lamb fighting off wolves whenever I had to walk to the stores. Grown men would prey on me. I would walk in silence and shame because they looked at me as if I was a grown woman. Looking back, I realized that most of those men knew, and didn't care, that I was just a child. I wanted to look like a kid, but there was no way to hide my physical appearance. In those moments I wanted to feel normal. I wanted to feel like a normal kid and not some seductive adult.

As years went by, I grew to love my looks. I became comfortable with the fact that I looked different than most. I learned to love me for who I was.

"Fill your life with adventures not things.
Have stories to tell, not stuff to show"
– From www.adventureinyou.com

From Where My Creativity Stems

As far as I can remember, playing dress up was my favorite thing to do. I would get so excited when Halloween would come around. I knew that it was the time when my mother would let me dress up as a princess. It was the time when I knew that I could put on makeup and put a costume together with things that I had at home. I don't remember a time when my siblings and I actually had a store-bought costume. All of our costumes were put together with things that we already had at home. We couldn't afford store-bought costumes, so we had to use our creativity and our imagination. I now see where my passion for putting things together creatively stems from—my younger years.

I remember one particular Halloween party from my youth when I was in kindergarten. The night before the Halloween party, I prepped my clothes and makeup that I was going to wear. That morning before going off to school, my mom made sure that I had everything that I needed. I wore regular clothes to school; I knew that if I wore my costume to school, that the mouths of the entire classroom would drop. Just before the party started, I asked my teacher if I could go in the restroom to change into my outfit. Once I changed clothes, sure enough, everyone's mouths had dropped. I had my hair down flowing past my shoulders. I wore one of my mother's dresses. I had on bold red lipstick, eyeliner, mascara, eye shadow, and blush. My teacher couldn't believe that I knew how to put on a full face of makeup as a child in kindergarten. I even painted my fingernails and rolled my hair with rollers the night before. There were other little girls trying to get me to do their makeup as well, but the teacher didn't allow me to do that.

Since my youth, Halloween has always been my favorite holiday. Every year I do something festive when it comes to putting together costumes. A few times, I've put together five costumes for one weekend of Halloween festivities. It has crossed my mind to become a wardrobe stylist. I'm pretty sure that if I wasn't doing the work that I currently do, that I would be a fashion stylist. I may consider getting into it later in life.

"Some days you just have to create your own shine."
From homeanquotes.com

The Realization of Being an Androgynous Woman

I watched a very popular film with my family in my younger years called "Boomerang". While watching the movie, one of the characters stood out the most to me. The character in the movie was named Strangé and played by Grace Jones. I remember people watching it laughing at her image. I didn't understand what the laughter was all about. There I was looking at who I thought was one of the most beautiful women that I had ever seen. I noticed her beautiful skin and her high cheek bones at first glance. I have high cheek bones as well. She had a stance that I had never seen before. Her legs were long and fit. Actually, her entire body was fit.

While watching, I didn't know the history behind her. I just knew that I was seeing a uniquely beautiful woman. She didn't look like most women that I grew up with or had even seen on TV. She didn't resemble any of my family members or family friends. She most definitely stood out. I noticed her strong facial features and her strong demeanor. I liked it. Strangé was very demanding in the movie. She put up a few verbal fights with some of the other characters in the movie. She was actually my favorite character in the movie. It wasn't due to the way she dressed. It was almost all in the way she showed strength and toughness. She went for what she wanted. Matter of fact, she demanded what she wanted. Her personality and her looks were strong. It took me until my adult years to realize how you define a woman of Strangé's characteristics. She was fit and feminine like a woman, but she also had similarities of what a man would be categorized by. Men are seen as strong and demanding in a lot of instances, personality wise and from a physical stand point. In Strangé I saw the physical and personality of a man. I also saw the physical and personality in her as a woman. I saw both female and male features in Strangé. I overheard someone bring up the term androgynous. I didn't know what the word meant, so I looked up the term and androgynous was defined by being partly male and partly female in appearance and of indeterminate sex.

Androgynous people are looked at as neither specifically feminine nor masculine. Years after watching the movie repeatedly, I realized that Strangé had a lot of similarities as I did. She was very bossy and aggressive; she showed sex appeal and beauty; she stood out. Her attire was much different from the rest of the cast. I have my own style of dress and people oftentimes tell me that I stand out. She took a stance on her feelings and what she expected from other cast members. I tend to express myself by demanding what I want and what I won't tolerate from people. I am a very aggressive woman. It's something that I've been dealing with since a young girl. I find that being aggressive is not always seen as a bad thing. I realize that some men find it a turn on to see women take a stand on their feelings. From my personal dating experience, I found that most men like aggressive women. In my opinion, most men are not attracted to women that they can push over or that would listen to their every demand. I call people who are pushovers "yes" men and women. Most men that I've come into contact with, whether it be family, friends, or random men that I meet, don't like "yes" women. Most of the women who are "yes" women usually get their feelings hurt and heartbroken more times than women who are not.

When I was a little girl, I often saw a few women in my family be strong in their words to the men that they dated. I thought that it was the women showing a sign of disrespect, but later in life I realized that it wasn't that at all. I feel that they didn't want to be looked at as a pushover in the eyes of their men. I picked up a lot of those characteristics as I grew into my womanhood. Going back to the movie "Boomerang" with the character Strangé, I appreciate the strength that she showed in the film. I learned some things from her. I know that it's perfectly fine to be who you actually are. It's much easier to accept and embrace the true self. It is too exhausting pretending to be someone else. It is a lovely thing to have those masculine and feminine traits all wrapped into one person. Strength shines and can be seen from miles and miles away.

"Don't change so people will like you. Be yourself and the right people will love the real you."
– Author Unknown

You Are NOT A Product Of Your Environment

I have never liked the phrase "You are a product of your environment." The reason why is because I am not much of what I have endured or witnessed growing up. My personality is much different than most people that I've grown up with or are even associated with. As a youth, I had people talk about me on several occasions and it would get back to me almost every time. I was told that I wouldn't finish high school, let alone receive a college degree and other certifications. I am guessing that because so many around me weren't completing school, they thought that I would not finish either. I was told that I would end up selling drugs. It was said that I would have a lot of "baby daddies" and a bunch of children that I wouldn't be able to tend to or take care of. I was told that no one would ever want to make me a wife because I was too "wild".

In the early years of elementary, I struggled with reading. In the beginning of my third grade year of school, I found out that there was a reading program. Some of my other classmates knew about this program as well. Most of the other kids who struggled like I did didn't want to sacrifice their playtime to go to the reading program. Some didn't feel that they needed the help, when in fact they needed it more than they could believe. Others had too much pride to ask for the help. Not me. I didn't feel prideful at all. I saw adults in my family struggle with their reading. I also have a family member that I was close to who is illiterate. I didn't want to see that for myself growing up. I have always been independent. I didn't feel comfortable asking others to read something for me. I wanted to read everything for myself. I wanted to know some of the basics when it came to reading. I wanted to know the difference between "to, two, and too". I wanted to know the difference between "your and you're". I wanted to differentiate "their, there, and they're". These are just a few examples of what I wanted to learn.

Once I signed up for that reading program, my whole world changed. I started reading every form of literature. I would read to my siblings and cousins on a regular basis. As they say, "Practice makes perfect." Sometimes I look back and think about where I would be in this world or if I would even be able to avenue through this world without that needed education. The way that a person grows up does not define how life will be once they reach adulthood.

"Someday everything will make perfect sense. So, for now laugh at the confusion, smile through the tears, and keep reminding yourself that everything happens for a reason."- Shinzoo

Filter Negative Energy:
Get It Away or Walk Away from It

It took me until my adult years to figure out this concept. For so long, I was used to bottling everything up if someone surrounded me with negative energy. Another way that I reacted towards it was with aggression. Neither of the two are positive ways to deal or cope with negative energy. At one point in my life, I thought that most people carried dark or negative energy. So many people walk around with hurt or anger built up inside of them, but I don't feel that most people are wired to be negative people. Life circumstances are sometimes causes of people being that way. It will take a person to actually realize that they are letting off negative energy if they want to find ways to let out the negative and bring about or let in the positive.

In my childhood and teenage years, it felt as if I was growing in negative energy. I did have some positive energies around me but it was very limited. So many people had that "hate the world" mentality. What I'm referring to is that they had many angers towards the world. Most times they would say that they disliked almost everything. I feel that some words can filter inside a person, especially a young child. Children tend to pick up words that are spoken from adults. I remember saying that I disliked certain foods because others around me didn't like those foods, even with me never trying or even tasting those particular foods. There were also certain hobbies that I found fascinating or interesting that I never tried because people didn't find them interesting. I played an instrument for six years of my life. I practiced almost daily until I perfected the sounds I was going for.

I was in the marching band for one year in high school. I loved playing music with the band. Some of my peers made fun of my uniform, telling me that I was too pretty for the uniform and that the band made me look "geeky". Those words set inside me. Shortly afterwards, I dropped out of the band. It was one of my biggest regrets. I wish that I had not let my peers influence me to drop out of the band. I was never the type to let others peer pressure me, which is why I felt that I had let myself down. I have always been in love with making and producing music, as well as listening to it. Looking back on it now, I realize that some of them were putting negative energy and negative vibes around me.

I also took an art class in high school. I had a passion for painting and drawing as well. My instructor couldn't believe that I had only taken one art class during my life at that time. The art instructor told me how he worked with many students and I was doing great with my art projects. I received some flack from other students about the teacher showing favoritism. One of the assignments that we were asked to draw were abstract objects. I chose to draw the front of a motorcycle. I've always been interested in vehicles. I received an "A" for my drawing. It was also chosen to be displayed in the hallway of the school. I was so proud of my work. Some of the other students weren't too happy about it. Some of them felt that they had more drawing experience and thought that their art pieces should have been chosen for display. Of course they were surrounding me with negative feedback when I should have been more encouraged to follow my artistic passions. Thankfully I didn't allow their negative feedback to keep me from exploring my artistic abilities. I took a few group art classes years later. On occasion, I even paint at home.

Painting and drawing requires many hours. With my down time being so limited, I'm not able to paint or draw as much as I would like to. When I do make time for my art projects, I feel so much more peaceful. I'm a strong believer that the moods of others can affect your mood. If someone's energy is dark or negative, then your mood can, in fact, change to his or hers even if you are in a positive state of mind. It's just like turning on or off a switch...it can change almost instantly. I literally try to surround myself around positive energy on a daily basis. If I wake up in a down mood, I will do a project that will uplift my spirit. I also know people who are always positive when I see or talk to them. Just like that light switch, my mood will switch from down and negative to uplifted and positive. I literally like to drown and play in positive energies. I have spent a large portion of my lifespan surrounded by negative energy. I refuse to spend the rest of my years in that dark place. My soul doesn't take negative energy well. Sometimes I can walk in a room with other people and the room can feel so heavy. As soon as I feel that energy, I will leave with little to no hesitation. I'm very open to my family and friends about only wanting to deal with positive energy. I physically feel sick if I'm in an uncomfortable situation or surrounded by negative energy.

In my opinion, a lot of people seem suppressed. I feel that many people lack laughter, smiles, and happiness. I also feel that sometimes it's my responsibility to make people laugh, smile, and find happiness. If I can help, I will help. If I try to lend a smile or put my positive energy around people and it is shunned away, then I will take a step back. I like authentic love and energy. If I feel that my energy is not wanted, I won't force it on someone. I just like happiness to be an element of energy most times. Some say that if everyone was bubbly or full of happiness that the world would be boring. I beg to differ on that idea. I feel that there would be much less hate, anger, and bitterness if more people embraced happiness. I always say surround yourself with positive people and positive energies. Sometimes it can mean avoiding "what you've always known." Sometimes people tend to stay around the same people that they've always grown up with or they have always known. For some, change can be heavy or difficult. I've heard people say, for instance, "Well, that's all I know" or "Well, that's all I've ever hung around." You have to tell yourself that sometimes change can be a good thing. For me, a change of environment from time to time is a must. It doesn't necessarily mean me packing up and going on a vacation. It can simply mean that I need to go for a walk, a bike ride, a hike, or any other type of adventure. At times, I will even redecorate the rooms in my home for an environmental change. Changing your home decor or office space can help reshape your mood. Sometimes you may need a break from hanging around the same people. It is okay to branch off and meet new people sometimes. New people can also mean new ideas. Bouncing off of ideas from new people can allow you to have new and fun events or ideas.

Branching off to meet new people has worked well for me. There's also a saying that says, "Your network is your net worth." I've found this to be very true. Some of my closest relationships are healthy for me personally, but for my professional life they aren't as healthy. You have certain people in your corner for specific reasons. Not everyone that you hang out with or that you are associated with are going to clique or vibe or connect with you on every level in your life. You will clash with certain things and certain areas of your life. Everyone's difference and interests make them unique. I've tried to not gravitate towards the same types of people. I like hanging around family, friends, and associates that have their own unique identity. Even with them having their own identity, we tend to have relatable interests in one or more areas of life. Where we differ, we can bounce off of each other in the areas that are either difficult for us to deal with or grasp. As long as the differences can be dealt with or handled properly or progressively in a positive manner, it can more than likely work for both sides. Being around other like-minded individuals can also give you peace of mind. The reason is because you can understand each other. When you can understand someone who thinks like you, you don't feel like you're alone in the world. Most people want to have compatibility—not just on an intimate level but also on a personal or business level.

"Train your mind to see the good in everything. Positivity is a choice. The happiness of your life depends on the quality of your thoughts." – Author Unknown

Making Yourself Your First Priority

I used to think that if I didn't put myself last, then I was being selfish. Most of my life, I put my needs and wants last. I used to make sure that my siblings were taken care of before I would do things for myself. I would put some things that I wanted on hold if I knew that my brothers or my mom were in need. Even when I was in college, if I had extra spending money and knew that there were things that my family needed back at home, I'd make sure that they had things before I did. This caused my life to be very heavy and caused me to be depressed. There were times that I wanted to do things just for myself, but I'd always feel guilty for thinking that way. I felt that I had to sacrifice everything if my household didn't have what they needed. In my mind, I felt that it was my responsibility to take care of my mom and siblings. My father wasn't in the picture, so I felt that I had to play that role since I was the oldest of my mother's children. Not only was I putting myself last on the home front with my mom and siblings, I was also putting myself last when it came to my marriage.

Growing up, I was used to traveling, spending a lot of time with friends and doing a lot of outdoor adventures. My husband was more of a homebody. After getting married, I only took a few trips each year. I stopped doing a lot of outdoor activities that I loved. I pretty much just did activities that I knew that he would enjoy. I look at my husband as my best friend, so I wanted to make sure that I did activities that would make him happy. Outside of family, I noticed that I was still putting myself last. I have always been involved in multiple activities and organizations. If I brought an idea to the table, oftentimes my ideas would be put on hold and others' ideas would be put on the forefront. I let a lot of my ideas be put to the wayside in order to make others more comfortable. In my mind, I was doing a good deed. I felt that I would be selfish if I didn't acknowledge others' first. It took me many years to internalize what was actually going on. I didn't realize until a few years ago how much I was hurting myself. I didn't realize how much of a burden I was putting onto my life. I was mentally drained. By me being mentally drained, it caused reactions to my physical being. I began to have facial breakouts from acne. I was eating my way through a lot of my stress and problems. This caused a lot of weight gain. Others around me did not really address the issue. I'm sure that they saw it, but probably didn't want to seem offensive. I would compare pictures of myself as I grew and evolved. A lot of times I didn't even recognize myself. I saw how much I had aged over the years. Most people would compliment me on how beautiful I was. It was hard for me to see what they were seeing. I saw a completely different being from what they were seeing. What I saw was exhaustion. I saw confusion. I saw a heavy-hearted and emotionally-weakened woman. I was tired… a lot. When I looked at pictures, I saw an internally much older woman with a younger woman's shell for a body. I never felt like my internal self ever matched my external self. Some would say that I look vibrant and youthful, but I rarely saw that. A few years ago, I walked past a full body mirror. I immediately started shedding tears. I was embarrassed by my reflection. I didn't even recognize myself. I rarely stopped to look at my "whole self". I didn't just see the image of myself in the mirror. I also saw the internal me—the side that very few were able to reach or see. Most people never even met the real me. I have shut most people out and prevented them from seeing the true and real me. I actually did that not just for my protection, but for theirs also. I primarily only wanted them to see the good in me. I wanted to make them as stress free as possible. I didn't want them to feel my emotions and feelings that I had battled with for so many years. I never wanted them to feel that intensity of pain. I knew that I had to find a way of releasing that built up hurt. I wanted to release it in a way that would be painless for others. I didn't want a cycle to be repeated.

The hurt that I felt also kept me from wanting to bear children. I didn't want to pass it on to any future children, so I decided that I didn't want to become a mother. I believe that energy can be transferred from one being to another. I figured that the world had enough pain and corruption, so why would I put that on an offspring? I remember telling myself that if the Creator gave me the option of being put on earth or to never have to exist, I'd rather not exist due to the amount of pain and hurt that I have been faced with. One day an amazing amount of strength came into me. I decided that I didn't want to live my life in hurt, shame, guilt, pity, stress, anxiety, depression, bitterness, exhaustion, or any other negative force of energy. I decided to go on a journey. I wanted to pull all of those negative energies out of me. I wanted to rebuild myself. I wanted to rebuild myself into how most people viewed me. I knew that it would be difficult, but I was ready for exploration. I was filled with excitement. I always believed in speaking things into existence so I knew that I could speak into existence my happiness. Feeling meaningful is something that I had always wanted. I reflected on what made me have happy moments as a child. Some of my favorite activities to do as a child were: reading, writing, art (coloring, painting, and drawing), dancing, playing softball, riding bicycles, and doing craft projects. In my eyes, age has no factor when it comes to things that you find as an interest. I decided to revisit those activities from my youth. In order to do these things, I knew that I was going to have to put myself before everyone else. My schedule and calendar were, most times, filled with things and activities that others needed help with. In the past, it rarely consisted of things that I wanted to do or found interest in. My schedule was primarily filled with activities that I was hosting/co-hosting for family events or organization events. I knew that I had to make a change. Whenever there are major changes, there are also emotions that will follow from others, including self. I knew that I would be faced with "growing pains". As you grow, whether it be physically or mentally, there will be some spurts of pain. Others will also endure some "growing pains". The pain that will come from self is primarily guilt.

In the beginning of my transition, I felt guilty for wanting to clear my schedule of other's activities to fit in time to do the activities that I wanted to do. I had to learn to say "no" to things that people wanted me to do. I knew that if I didn't turn down some activities, that I wouldn't be able to make time for myself. I lost a lot of people that used to surround themselves by me. It took me to take care of myself to realize how much I was being used by people. If I wasn't doing things that were beneficial for and to them, they didn't want to stick around. Some people got angry with me when I refused to put their activities on my calendar. Most times they literally wanted nothing else to do with me. Once I did my "sweep" of clearing my schedule to make time or room for myself, I looked up and there were only a few people that were still around. I do remember my mother telling me when I was a teen that I thought that everyone was my friend and they were actually not. I have also been called gullible a few times in my life because I had so much hope in people. I try so hard to see the good in people, but more often than not many seem to let me down. I feel that I've been taken for granted numerous times. Even though I have been let down many times, I still try to look past the flaws in people and see primarily the good in them. Getting over those growing pains were tough. With any transition there will be changes on your body and in your mental. I had to mentally wrap my mind around the concept that I didn't just want this change, but I actually needed the change. I knew that if there was no change with putting myself first, that I wouldn't be any good to anyone else. I had to be a strong person. In order to help others or be there for others, you have to be there for yourself...first. Over a short period of time, it actually got easier for me to say no to things that I didn't want to do. I no longer saw it as me being selfish. I felt that it would be selfish of me to take on responsibilities that I knew I didn't want to do and then slack on doing those things. I felt that it would be wasting my time and their time because my heart wouldn't be in it.

"Life isn't about finding yourself.
Life is about creating yourself"
- George Bernard Shaw

Your Rest (Mental, Physical, and Spiritual) Can Be Your Safe Haven

It took for others to tell me to slow down at times before I actually would. From childhood I was used to always being on the move. We were either in after-school programs or we were at the houses of friends and relatives. On the weekends we watched very little television. When the weather was nice, we would spend several hours a day being outdoors. Needless to say, it was almost embedded in me to be up and about most of the week. Most of my life my body has not really known how to rest. I have worked most of my life, having held a job since the age of 12, and I have never been laid off. Education, work, and activities were pretty much all that I knew. All of these things helped me to stay sane. Staying busy was my safe haven, so I thought. It all caught up to me years after college.

I noticed the "yo-yo" effect of my physical weight. I would fluctuate between 50 lbs. of weight throughout my adult years. It was primarily due to the lack of my mind and body resting and eating improper meals because I was always on the go. I also know that depression played a part as well. My mind was constantly wandering and thinking of past events. I always had a concern for my family and friends. I took on a lot of their burdens because I was pretty much their safe haven. Your body will make you slow down even when you don't want to slow down. I had to tell myself that it was okay to have rest time and rest days. When you rest, it actually helps cleanse your organs and help prevent premature aging. Resting helps strengthen your immune system. It helps relieve your mental edge. I was noticing that my sleep was often interrupted when I didn't give my body the adequate amount of rest that it needed. My lack of rest caused me to be moodier, and I would get angry and irritated often. Being restless and irritable took too much out of me. I knew that I had to work on things within myself. It is not cute walking around with a frown on your face. I feel more appreciated and at peace when I have a smile on my face and laughter in my heart. Yoga became a part of my life as well. It allowed me to rest my mind and filter out thoughts that were stressing me out. It made me more flexible and it helped me focus on my posture and my breathing. Sometimes I would go for a walk on my breaks on lunch. That allowed me to rest my thoughts also. I realized that rest doesn't necessarily mean sleep. You have to take rest breaks throughout the day along with getting adequate sleep.

*"Life is much brighter when we focus on what truly matters" -
Author Unknown*

There Has to Be More to
This Thing Called LIFE

I knew that there was more to the life that I grew up in once I discovered books. Thankful for the R.I.F. program, a free book program through Grand Rapids Public Schools. That's where I fell in love with anthropology and history. Of course, I didn't know what anthropology was as a youth, which is the study of human societies and cultures and their development. I knew that there was more outside the city of Grand Rapids. I have a fascination with learning about how others live. I was always consumed with my way of living and navigating through life. I'm sure that my constantly having to be in tune with myself caused a spark with me wanting to know how others lived.

One group of people that I learned about in college was the Yanomami Tribe. They are an isolated tribe in South America. They reside in the mountains and rainforests in parts of Venezuela and Brazil. I became fond of them because they had to hide some of their deepest emotions. It was taboo for this tribe to speak on death; this may still be the case. One of the ways they avoided speaking of the death was to not bring up the name of the deceased. They were able to not bring up the names of the deceased because they had birth names that were less likely to have to be used again. For example, a person would be named "Monkey Nail" or another name that didn't have to be used in a day-to-day conversation. Often, I like to watch documentaries and watch National Geographic shows, where I learn about different people and their cultures. I love to visit more parts of the world. I would like to travel outside the states more often to see what's out there.

"Get outside everyday. Miracles are waiting everywhere." – Author Unknown

It Ain't Easy Being Cheesy

When I was a young teen, I would get advice from family and my family's friends about the dating life. One particular conversation has always stuck with me that I had with one of my relative's friend. He told me that he cared about me and didn't want to see me go down the wrong path. He mentioned that he always wanted to see me carry myself like a lady. He was always blunt when with me when we talked. I never saw him as trying to pry into my personal life, but was actually trying to give me some positive guidance on life. I somewhat saw him as an uncle since he was around the family so much. I actually loved when people gave me words of wisdom. It sticks to me more than people realize. One day he told me, "Young lady, it's not easy being cheesy." I looked at him with this puzzled look and started laughing. I thought he meant that it wasn't easy to smile. He meant something completely different than what I was thinking. He then said, "Do you know what I mean by that?"

"Yeah, it's not easy to smile... right?" I answered.

"Well no. No, that's not what I meant." He then proceeded to walk over to the couch, spread his legs wide open and said again, "It's not easy being cheesy."

I looked at him with surprise. I then realized it was not a laughing matter. In fact, it was one of his life lessons he was telling me. After he made this gesture, he said, "I've seen a lot of people abuse sex and I don't want you to abuse it. Take care of your body. You are a beautiful young lady and I want these knuckle heads out here to respect you. I want you to go to school and get your education. Babies can wait."

After he said that, my smile went away and I responded with, "okay."

"If you have to use your assets for his attention, then chances are you will be ass out of his life real quick. But...carry on if you must."
- Toni Rain

My Maternal Grandfather and Grandmother

I've only seen good in my grandfather. He always took care of his family...not just his wife and kids, but all of his many grandchildren. I've never once seen him argue with my grandmother or try to belittle her. I've never seen my grandmother work a day in her life while I was growing up. She was well taken care of by her husband. In fact, my grandfather also took in one of my uncles that my grandmother had and raised him as if he was his own. I didn't even know about this until I was much older. My grandfather never treated my uncle as if he was any different from his biological children.

One of the most vivid things that I remember about my grandfather is that he would usually be the first to awaken on the weekends. It always seemed like I was the second to arise in the mornings, following after my grandfather. In their kitchen, there was a large white porcelain sink. Above the sink was a large window with white curtains. In the early mornings on the weekends, my grandfather would fill the kitchen sink with hot bubbly dish water. The window above the sink was opened as far as it could be opened. The curtains were pulled all the way to the sides so that the bright sun could shine bright into the kitchen. On those mornings, the wind would blow really hard causing the curtains to sway from side to side. I remember the cool crisp morning air coming in through the windows. I still remember how the air felt upon my face. Some days the air would cause me to get goosebumps, but it didn't bother me. I actually looked forward to it. He would then fill the sink with dishes that were left out from the night before. Our family is huge and we would have family gatherings at their house every weekend. While he would fill the sink with dishes, I would always help him. I actually liked playing with the suds more than anything. When I washed the dishes, I made sure to get every spot off, so that they could be perfectly clean.

Once the dishes were cleaned, then came time to clean the rest of the kitchen. I would help him sweep and mop the floor. After all the cleaning was done, I would watch him prepare breakfast for each person that was in the house. I primarily saw him get breakfast prepared on his days off from work. When I say each person, I'm referring to his wife, a few of his children, some of his grandchildren, and some of the neighborhood friends. There was always at least 10 people in the house on a daily basis. The house was always busy, but was filled with so much love and laughter. So, while my grandfather would cook, the others in the house would rise one after the other. My grandfather was an amazing cook. The breakfast would have the entire house smelling of delicious food. My favorite food item that I loved for him to make were grits with butter and a few sprinkles of salt and pepper. I also enjoyed his homestyle potatoes. His food was always flavorful. You could taste the love in all the food that he made. In almost everything he cooked, he would put onions and green peppers in it. I think that's where my love for spices and vegetables come from. As everyone started to awake, they'd all come to the kitchen to see what he had prepared. We'd all make our plates and sit around and talk in the living and dining rooms. A lot of times my grandfather was quiet. He would just be observant. He'd look up, make eye contact, and just smile. He had such a shy and bashful smile.

He expressed joy by giving many smiles and grins. He wasn't a man of many words. Most times when he spoke, it was in regards to his thinning hair. He had a large bald spot at the top of his head. He would always jokingly say to me, "Can you put me a big ponytail in the middle of my head please? I need you to put all this hair in a ponytail." I always giggled at that. He knew that he didn't have enough hair for me to do that. Then he'd say, "Well, since you can't put a ponytail there, can you just comb or brush my scalp?" I'd get a comb and brush and comb his scalp. Every time I'd comb his hair, he'd drift into a sleep. It made him feel so relaxed. Looking back, I realize how tired he must've been. He worked hard inside and outside the home. He did jobs that were physically draining on his body and especially on his feet. His feet ached so much daily and he would just work through the pain. Sometimes I'd get a bucket and fill it with hot water and Epsom salt. It helped him to relax and enjoy the little down time that he had.

As an adult, I have even more respect for my grandfather, knowing how much he sacrificed for our family. I realized that he wasn't selfish at all. I never really saw him have a lot of down or personal time for himself. Not many people are built mentally or physically the way he was. In my eyes, it seemed as if the entire world was on his shoulders. I don't know many men who would sacrifice most of their free time or most of their income for their family. I only know of a handful of men like that. Growing up, I even had an allowance from my grandparents. They took great care of me. My grandmother taught me about life at a young age. She taught me about racism and how the world operated. I was filled with wisdom early on, which is my reasoning for always having an old soul. My grandmother also taught me about wearing proper undergarments. I even learned from my grandmother how a lady is supposed to slow dance. She taught me how to paint my fingernails. My grandmother had the most beautiful natural fingernails that I had ever seen on a woman. They were long, thick, and always manicured. She had a collection of fingernail polish of many different colors. Most of the colors were earth toned. When I was in elementary I used to always like it when she would run her beautiful nails across my face and neck to tickle me. It was one of her ways of showing love to me. She would slowly and softly glide her nails across my face and neck and I would giggle and smile with my eyes closed while she did this. When I opened my eyes, she would be looking at me with a lit up beautiful smile in return. Of course, I would ask her to continue to do this.

I learned very early on about femininity from my grandmother. She was the first person to teach me that women should wear skirts and dresses. I was also taught about slips and how they should always be worn if your clothes were see-through. My mom never really wore makeup other than eye makeup or lipstick. My grandmother was the one to teach me about foundation and concealer. She told me that whenever I was old enough to wear it, to make sure that my makeup matched my skin complexion. She was against me wearing a lot of it. I was told how after a while of wearing makeup, that it could cause damage to my skin. She complimented me on how beautiful I was all the time. She told me to always take great care of my skin. My grandmother battled with skin issues, so she didn't want me to go through the same things. Most of the girls in the family admired her femininity. All of the women learned a thing or two from my grandmother on how to be a woman.

She also had a sense of humor that was out of this world. She would have me laughing hard all of the time. She reminded me of Delores from the movie Harlem Nights. She would tell a person off but also love on them at the same time. Whenever I was around her, it was like I was walking into a "no-mess zone". She did not put up with disrespect at all. She was a very strong intellectual woman. My grandmother was also observant. She was very outspoken about almost everything. She didn't allow people to run over her. I actually looked up to her most because of that. She showed me strength. I've seen her break people down with her words. In all honesty, I picked up that trait from her. I'm loving for the most part, but whenever I'm disrespected or backed into a corner, I tend to break people down with my words also. As a child, I was called grown a lot because I would pick up words that the adults used. Sometimes I didn't know what I was saying, but I did use them in the right context. Kids used to often say, "You aren't grown. You can't talk to me like that. I don't have to listen to you." Looking back, I realized how bossy I was and how I can still be bossy. I saw how my grandmother ran her household and put order in how she wanted people to act and behave. I know that I'm the same way, and I get a lot of my ways from my grandmother. I miss her so much. I'll continue to keep some of those life lessons and words of wisdom within me. She will always continue to live through me.

"When you want something with all your heart that's when you are closest to the soul of the world. It's always a positive force." – From "The Alchemist"

The Gaze in My Grandmother's Eyes

I remember her eyes more than anything. The most vivid memory that I have of my maternal grandmother is that she often sat at her dining room table. So many times, I wondered what she was thinking or what was going on in her mind. I remember her being in her thoughts. She would have her body sitting at an angle on her chair. Her arms would lay over her knees with her hands intermingled together, slightly between her knees. She would tap her feet lightly to the floor, alternately looking up. She was a fan of blues music. Some of her favorite artists were Betty Wright, Johnny Taylor, and BB King. She would sit in her chair for hours at a time listening to her music with a gazing look. I wondered if she was truly happy. Was she sad? Was she just being? Was she just in the moment? I was always told, "Stay in a child's place and stay out of grown folk's business" by my family members. Because of that, I never asked how or what she was feeling. I've always been wise beyond my years. I was able to pick up on things and read people's body language at a young age. I was one of the kids that wanted to know everything. I would question my mother about everything. I had a question for almost every question that I had. I would sometimes get on adults' nerves because I always had multiple questions for them.

I remember one of my aunts telling my mother that it was good that I asked so many questions because it would help me to be smarter. Looking back, I'm glad that I was inquisitive. It helped me get through this life. I was able to depend on myself for things that I needed to know and be prepared for later on in life. Looking back, I was also able to figure out why my grandmother had that gazing look in her eyes. She was tired during that time. She didn't really take breaks and make time for herself. She was constantly surrounded by people. I've never seen my grandmother by herself. There was usually someone around. I never once saw her take a vacation. I rarely saw her leave from the house. I've never seen her once leave the house alone. She was attached to her family. She loved her grandchildren, many of whom she took care of and even raised, along with her children. That's more than enough to make someone tired. I've never known her to be employed, but she was always doing something around the house or entertaining people at the house. As a matter of fact, I have very little history of Grandmother and how she was in her youth and younger years of her womanhood. I wish that I had asked more questions of her. I want to know more about her life. I want to know if it was easy or hard growing up as a young woman. I want to know where she got her femininity from. I'm sure that she received it from my great-grandmother, her mother. I just wish that I was able to hear about her life from her.

There were so many times I wanted to ask and learn more. I was afraid that I would get turned down from asking questions. With me having a love for history, I wish that I had more of it. I want to be able to pass it down to the little girls in my family. I want them to know where and what they come from. I believe in our ancestors being able to speak to us. There are signs of them around us. Sometimes they come to us in our dreams. My grandmother has come to me on several occasions in my dreams. I would privately cry to myself while taking a shower. Sometimes it would even be while I was working, with my back turned away from my coworkers, so they didn't notice anything. Internally I had so much pain in my soul and in my heart from missing her so much after she passed. I knew that our family events would never be the same. I knew that I wasn't going to be able to pass down my purses that she always wanted whenever I would visit her. At times I couldn't understand her since she struggled with her speech after she had her stroke. I would still listen to her laugh and watch her smile. I understood her facial expressions. Most times she still had a smile on her face, so I knew that whatever she was saying was something good. While I was growing up, she was also silly and a jokester. I loved her sense of humor. I held on to those memories to help me get through those moments of missing her. Sometimes those memories weren't enough to hold me up.

One dream that I had of my grandmother was very vivid. It was shortly after her death that I had a breakdown from missing her so much. In the dream, I walked on the porch of the house her and my grandfather lived in while I was growing up. My grandfather opened the door. He smiled at me and said not one word. As I walked in, my grandmother was sitting on a couch. In front of her was a coffee table. On the coffee table were many pictures of women in our family. I looked at the pictures but didn't pay much mind to them. She had a straight stern look on her face when I looked up at her. She had the look of disappointment on her face. She said, "Look at this." She looked down on the table at the pictures as she said that. I looked at the pictures again then looked back at her. She said, "Do you see this?"

I responded, "See what?"

She mentioned how she was looking at the strong women that she raised. She told me that she raised strong women. She said that I was strong too. "I raised you better than that. Get it together. Do you hear me?" In my dream, I just started balling my eyes out after she said that to me. I knew exactly what she was referring to. She wanted me to be strong for my family as she was strong for our family. I feel that her spirit knew that I was having a hard time without her being around. She was speaking life and strength back into me through my dreams. Since then I have become a much stronger woman for my family and I owe it all to her.

"I've seen better days, but I've also seen worse. I don't have everything that I want, but I do have all I need. I woke up with some aches and pains, but I woke up. My life may not be perfect, but I am blessed." - Zenith Quotes; Lessons Learned in Life

I Watched My Grandfather
Take His Last Breath

It was a tough journey for my grandfather. He was battling illnesses that were literally taking over his body. One illness led to another. Most of the times that I saw him, I saw his smile first. There was a time I went to pay him a visit. It was shortly after he received his amputation. He had lost one of his legs, partially due to an infection. I was standing outside the facility. One of the nurses brought him out to see us. As they rolled him out in his wheelchair, he had his head down. I said, "Hey Granddad, how are you?" He looked up at me. All I saw was a blank look of despair. Of all the times I've seen him, it was the first time that I saw this particular facial expression. It literally hurt my soul.

He was such an amazingly beautiful person. Of all the times that he had been there to comfort me, I wasn't able to fully be able to comfort him. I smiled at him, having that little bit of hope that he would smile back at me. He didn't. His eyes were set on mine. His eyes said so many things. He let me know that it was time. I knew that deep down inside of me, that it was time for me to get prepared to say my goodbyes. Shortly after that day, I received a phone call to come to the hospital. His condition had worsened. When I arrived at the hospital, there were many of my family members present. I had already prepared my mind, body, and spirit for what I would be walking into. I saw him lying in the bed. He looked very frail and restless. I went over and just started to gently rub the sides of my hands against his face. I could hear everyone talking amongst themselves. I knew that they were trying to distract themselves of what was to come. I remember seeing him trying to breathe. His chest moving up and down gasping for air. I could tell that it was difficult and painful for him to catch a breath.

We were there for hours. I went out of the room for a moment to talk amongst family, get a few laughs in, and to comfort them. Something struck me inside and told me to go back in the room to visit my grandfather. Shortly after I went back in, that's when it happened. I saw him take a few more short breaths, then they stopped. The people he loved the most were with him. I watched my grandfather take his last breath the day before former President Barack Obama was first elected as president. I'm sure that he would have wanted to witness that monumental moment.

"Grandchildren don't stay young forever, which is good because Pop-pops have only so many horsey rides in them." - Gene Perret

Sometimes It's Not Him or Her Sometimes It's You

When was the last time you brought adventure into the relationship? When was the last time you initiated a spark? Boring is simply that—boring. I'm not a relationship expert by far, but I sure do know about an adventure or two. Adventures don't always cost money either. Have you had an adventure in your living room, dining room, or on one of your staircases? If not, I think that you should consider it. Have you ever had a picnic with your significant other in your backyard or even your actual place of residence? You'd be surprised by how you'd both enjoy it. Just like you want to be loved and cherished, so do most other people. I feel that the love you want to be lavished onto you, you should put that same love and energy into another person—especially your significant other.

When was the last time you wrote your lover a love note? When was last time you prepared them their favorite dish or dessert that they love so much? Even if you don't know how to make their favorite dish or dessert, have someone you know that's an amazing cook or pastry chef prepare it for them. It doesn't necessarily have to be prepared by you. Just the thought alone that you were thinking about them will make the favor worth their while. It's up to you to find the trinkets of what their heart desires, just the same as it being up to them to find your trinkets. There's a song by Musiq Soulchild that's called "Teach Me How to Love". I studied the lyrics to that song. Some people actually don't know how to love or sometimes how they love may not be familiar to you. Perhaps their style of showing love or even making love to you is something that you've never experienced. The same could also be in regards to you as well. Maybe they've never experienced your style of love. Do you believe in role playing or cosplay? I personally love cosplay. I feel that life should be lived in fun. I also like to play dress up. It puts a spark in my life. I also believe that you're never too old to play dress up. In my eyes, dress up is not just for children. Find out the desires, needs, and wants of your significant other. It's okay to ask. I'd prefer to be with someone who studies me and wants to learn about me. I feel that it's part of their responsibility as much as it is mine to study them.

It really does take some studying and following up when it comes to getting to know someone. Even if you've been with someone for years, you both consistently change and evolve over those years. My interests sometimes change every year to every few years. Some people say that I want to try almost everything when it comes to adventures or hobbies. It took me many years to realize that I had to cater to my significant other just as much as I wanted them to cater to me. I didn't want to soak up all the energy and leave them with nothing. If you want love, then you also have to be love.

"What women should know: A man who truly loves you will never let you go no matter how the situation is. What men should know: A woman who truly loves you will be angry at you for so many things, but will stick around." - Phenlee Humbler, sayingimages.com

Changing The Wrapper Of The Candy

We, as human beings, can get caught up in the idea of changing a person. If we're in a relationship and the other person seems a little rough around the edges, we often try to smooth out those edges. We try to change that person by telling them how we want them to dress around certain people. We ask them to speak a certain way or in a certain tone. We oftentimes try to mold them into who we want them to be. I had a habit of doing this with guys that I dated in my younger years. Looking back, I see that I wasn't letting them be their true selves. I was trying to dress them up or "change the wrapper of the candy" without even noticing it. Even if I asked them to change the way they did things or changed the way they dressed, in reality, I still had that same "piece of candy" deep down inside. Changing the "wrapper" of someone does not change the person inside.

I learned that you truly can't change anyone. Most times they will change or evolve on their own...but only if they want to. It actually grinds my gears when someone tries to force or want me to change into something or someone that I'm not. I've been told that I'm eclectic and eccentric. I love the fact that I have various styles of dress. I love the fact that I can mix and mingle with just about anyone or any group of people. I love the fact that I've been with people from all different walks of life. It makes me feel powerful that I can be who I am without anyone trying to change the wrapper of me. For the most part, I don't recall anyone that I've ever dated trying to change the true person that I am. In fact, I feel that they embraced my unique self. Looking back, I should have never tried to change who they were. Once I noticed what I was doing, I quickly changed that about myself. I don't consider myself a programmer when it comes to computers or people. I will no longer try to program anyone into being who I want them to be. I want them to be their true selves.

"Let your smile change the world, but don't let the world change your smile."
- Author Unknown

Bootsy Collins' Interview On
The Questlove Show: Catfish

One day I was on my lunch break. I received a notification for The Questlove Show, which was playing on Pandora. I opened the link to hear the show. The musical artist that was being interviewed was Bootsy Collins. He is from Cincinnati, Ohio. Cincinnati is recognized as the Funk Capital for many bands. Bootsy was talking about his upbringing. One thing that stood out the most about that interview was him speaking about how he and his family made the struggle fun. He said that he didn't take ownership of the hardships. Sometimes you have to make light of situations that can be emotional. Bootsy and his family filled their home with music and laughter. He looked up to his older brother Catfish who was eight years older than he was. He wanted approval of his brother. Bootsy finally got that moment from his brother once he played back up bass for him. From that day on, Bootsy continued to play with Catfish.

When the interviewers asked Mr. Collins about playing for or with other artists, he mentioned how he often didn't remember the songs that he played. He said, "I was never interested in what I've done prior. I was interested in what was coming next." He mentioned how he didn't have enough time to focus and look back on his music. His life moved fast. He talked about how if someone brought up a song he did, he would ask them to play it for him. Mr. Collins said that music was able to take them out of a particular place. For him, he mentioned, "It's like looking in a mirror and laughing at yourself. Once I got on a path...I started listening to the universe and what they'd tell me to do. That's what I was feeling."

"Before Alice got to Wonderland, she had to fall."
– From inspirationalquotesmagazine.com

Getting Married So Young

I met the man that I later came to marry when I was 21 years old. When I first saw him, I was just coming to the end of a previous relationship. I wasn't in a good space and wasn't interested in dating anyone seriously. At the time, my husband and I were college students. He noticed me before I even made eye contact with him. From what I was told, it was love at first sight for him. The day that he noticed me, I was coming from a gym workout. I had on a jogging suit about to head to my next class. During the course of the semester, I noticed this guy who would walk past my class each week. As he would walk past, he'd quickly take a glance and continue walking to his class. He did this each week for the school year. I was a student worker on campus at the counselor's office in the building where we took the majority of our classes. The last week of the school semester, my friend invited me out to a night club. I wasn't in the mood to party at all. She pretty much begged me to go out. I was bribed into going because she had VIP tickets and didn't have anyone else to go out with. As soon as we got into our section at the club, I noticed the guy who walked past my classroom each week. I looked over and I could see him whispering to one of his friends while looking up at me.

For me, it was a little awkward since he would just look at me and never speak or approach me. Later on that evening, I went down to the lower level of the club and stood by the dance floor. He finally approached me and began to talk to me. He then asked if I wanted to dance. Come to find out, we were both great dancers. We flowed to the music so well. After we danced, he asked for my phone number. I declined but I proceeded to ask for his instead. He said that he wasn't expecting me to call him. In fact, I called him the same night and left a voicemail. The next morning, he returned my call and asked me if I wanted to go out on a date with him. I declined the offer. I told him that I'd stay in touch over the summer break by phone. He checked up on me consistently throughout the summer. Even though I wasn't interested in being in a relationship, he was consistent with checking up on me and making sure that I was enjoying my summer.

Once I returned for my senior year of college after my summer break, he offered his assistance with me unpacking my things. When I got settled into the school year, I had car troubles and was using public transportation. I also used public transportation when I had to get groceries for my apartment. He didn't like me walking from the bus stops to my apartment with many bags. He offered to take me grocery shopping and helped me with taking me to run my errands. As a gesture of my appreciation for him looking after me, I prepared him dinner after my classes. We began to grow closer in our friendship. We even had a class together and were going to school to pursue the same degree. Our upbringings were so different. Our personalities were different as well. Ironically, we had never crossed paths prior to our junior years of college. In all honesty, I thought that he was a transfer student. He kept a low profile, which attracted me the most about him. I was friends with a lot of the athletes and fraternity guys. I would sit and listen to how they talked about women, which made me afraid to date anyone I went to college with. We began dating some months into our senior year of college.

Things moved pretty quickly after that. He proposed a few months after we graduated from college. We were so young and just now experiencing our adulthood. It was a scary time in life for me. All I knew was school and working hard. I also didn't have a lot of respect for men at that time. I was very attached to my family. I knew that my family was looking up to me to find a successful career and to be able to help the family more financially. I had people pressuring and asking me when we were going to start a family. I had my mind made up that I only wanted success and stability. As much as I love children, I wasn't in a rush to have any. I was content with helping my family out with their children. I made my husband aware of this before we got married in the case he was planning on having children. The man that I was soon to marry and I were engaged for about eight months before we got married. We often times got into it. I was still trying to find myself. He was still trying to find himself. I used to question if I made the right decision. I used to question, "Did we move too fast?" "Are we too young for marriage?" Is this what marriage is supposed to look like?"

There were only a few examples of marriage that I had seen. Not many people in my family were married. Only a few of my friends were married and they too were just experiencing it. I am stubborn and prideful and didn't really want to ask for advice. I thought that I should be able to handle things on my own. I knew so many people were looking up to me. There were also a lot of people looking down on me and wanting me to fail. I was often looked at as the girl who had it all. I was always popular. What a lot of people didn't realize was that I was also under a lot of pressure. I was dealing with those deep internal hurts that I was so easily able to hide. Oftentimes, I turned that hurt into anger towards my husband. I had two sides to me. I was this peaceful flower child, then other times, I was very violent. My husband also had issues with aggression and violence. He had two sides to him as well. He could be quiet on one end, then violent the next. Whenever I got upset, I was quick to walk away or leave the house to control my aggression. Even though we argued and fought, we loved each other even harder.

There was a period where my husband and I separated. Separation was needed for the both of us. Many people knew about it, but there were some that didn't know. We both went through counseling separately. I believe it helped us see things more clearly. I feel that some people look at counseling as being taboo. I found it to be helpful. My hope is that couples become more comfortable with their relationship styles. Even with the misfortunes during the marriage, finding love and friendship is what allows it to be much healthier. Even through that period, we still remained friends. The strength of our friendship is what kept us strong throughout our separation. We were able to find that medium to reunite. The saying, "Love conquers all" is so real to me. I never knew that I could love someone so much. Even if my husband and I never got back together, I already knew that no other man would be able to fill the space of love that I had for him. When you go through storms such as the ones we went through, you really do see how others look at you or feel about you deep inside. During our separation, we were both in a dark place. One thing that surprised me was that many of my family and friends gave us both support to reunite with each other. There were also some family members that I found who despised us being together from the very beginning of our relationship. Whenever they're around, I smile as if I don't know a thing. It is their problem… not ours.

I'm thankful that my husband and I have a strong companionship. We could look at each other from across the room and know exactly what each other is thinking or feeling. Most importantly, I'm thankful for our friendship. It's so hard to find and have genuine friendships. So many people have artificial personalities. Many people say that I'm blunt or "too real". I personally like that quality about myself. I want people to see the real me. I don't want people to see the watered-down version of me. I always try to be respectful to people, even when I'm expressing myself. During our separation, we were open with dating other people. We actually talked about some of the people we were seeing. It's more common in marriages than people are willing to admit or even talk about. He was more uncomfortable with the idea than I was. For those that didn't know that we were in an open relationship, they would slander our names. Eventually I was able to get over that fact. I learned to live for me and not for others.

"I should be through with love, but there's a God up above that keeps saying 'Betty try...don't give up...you know why? The sun is gonna shine, cause you are mine (all mine). You just keep doing your best and I will do the rest. Cause I love you Betty like I do.'" - "After the Pain" by Betty Wright

Women Can Shine Together

The song "Diamonds" by Rihanna comes to mind when I think of walking in purpose and power. The thought of the song makes my body stand up straight. It uplifts my spirit. Even though it's considered a love song, I hear the lyrics much differently than most people. I hear it as an empowerment song. I mentally envision positive energy of people coming together and standing strong together. I love being around other strong people. I need people that can pick me back up whenever I'm feeling low. Most times I can recognize another strong person. I can especially see another woman who displays signs of strength. Some women are intimidated by other strong women, but I actually embrace it. We can all be happy and powerful together. We can all shine and sparkle together.

It's so often that I hear that women can't get along. I actually embrace being around other women. It's not always a receptive experience towards me, but I don't give up on working or being around other women. I'm unsure of where we lost those female connections. The older I get the smaller circles of women I see. There should be more uplifting amongst women. There are so many more of us then there are men in this world. We have to make it work. I don't have the answers to fix it, but I'll continue to do my part. For the most part, I try to contribute by bringing young girls and women together by hosting events that empower us. One of my favorite things to do is host tea parties with my nieces. I want to help mold them to see that girls/women can have fun and love on each other. I want them to see that there is a need for women to practice embracing one another instead of breaking each other down. We have to realize how powerful we are. Yes, we can be a force alone, but we have more strength when we work together. I have a relationship with some of my childhood friends because they too have that same feeling. We had very few arguments or disagreements and we realized that we were better with each other.

"The world is a canvas. We use our thoughts, our presence, and our creativity to portrait our paintings."
- Toni Rain

Missing My College Years

I was told to hold onto my years of being in college. I was told that they would be the best years of my life. Looking back, I couldn't agree more. I was the student in the dorm who brought most of the entertainment. Many of my friends and some of my relatives would come to visit me, especially during my freshman year of college. I was the one who brought the guys for the female residents of my dorm. Most of my family consist of males. I like to see people having fun and I enjoy bringing people together. My friends and family would always bring food and snacks for us. This helped us out a lot, especially when most of us had limited food.

There were some crazy, yet fun, things that happened while I was in college. One of the events that stands clear in my mind, was being involved in a police chase. Yes...I was in a police chase. Most people who know me wouldn't even think of me being involved in anything like that. In actuality, I was "accidentally" involved. Some of my campus friends and I were connected to some of the local residents around the city. We were freshman and naive to a lot of things that people would be involved in. One evening, my campus friends and I were invited to the residence of one of our local friends. My campus friends and I didn't have a vehicle, so one of my local friends volunteered to pick us up to come to their place. It was snowing out that evening. There was black ice on the pavement. Our local friend came to our dorm to pick us up and we headed to their place. As our local friend was driving, they noticed that the police were trailing us. They mentioned how they didn't have a license and how they weren't going to go to jail. Eventually the police turned on their sirens. Our local friend began driving faster and faster. My friends and I were terrified. We were asking them to stop the car. They refused and began to drive even faster.

Now, mind you, it was in the winter with snow and black ice everywhere. I remember gripping different parts of the car while my heart was racing so fast. I didn't want us get in a car accident, first and foremost, and I didn't want us all to go to jail. The driver eventually drove all the way to their house while the police was following us. Once we arrived at the house, the driver jumped out of the car and ran off. The police surrounded the vehicle we were in and started asking us many questions which most we were unable to answer. They asked to see all of our IDs. From the different addresses, they saw that we weren't permanent residents of the area. That actually saved us from getting in trouble from the law. We explained how we were picked up to attend a party and how we were in college. I remember that night so vividly. Never would I think that I'd ever be in a police chase. Looking back on that moment, it is surreal. My friends from college and I occasionally talk about that evening. It still blows our minds. We were just so happy that we didn't get into any legal troubles.

The ladies that I was with that evening were a part of some really fun times together through our college years. We would even spend our Sundays having breakfast and attending events outside of seeing each other during the week. I looked forward to us hanging out regularly. They were my family away from home. It's nice that some of us still stay in contact. I actually stay in contact with many of my childhood friends as well. I value friendships and I don't take them lightly. It was also fun visiting friends in different dorms. Outside of wanting to link up with friends in the different dorms, we also enjoyed having other food options. Most of the times, the food menus varied in the dorms. The cafeteria of the dorm that I was in my freshman year of college was popular for offering stir fry options. A lot of people came to the dorm to eat. They also enjoyed the company of me and my friends because we were so much fun to be around. I remember the George Foreman grill was popular around that time. We also used to make meals from our grills in the kitchenette. We would have two to three Foreman grills going at the same time and make healthy meals for each other. Even though we liked to eat, we made sure to incorporate some healthy foods in our eating habits. We were told about the "Freshman Fifteen", so we wanted to stay as healthy as we could.

I miss working out with my old college friends at the recreational center. The dorm where we stayed in had many hills. We used to walk up those hills, which, at the time, felt like we were hiking up mountains. It helped us stay in shape. People called us the "Valley Girls" because of where we were staying on campus. I also miss our movie nights. Almost every time it was my turn to choose the movie, I would pick my #1 favorite movie, which is "Love Jones". I not only love that movie, but I also love the soundtrack to the movie. I still watch it each and every year.

"College inspired me to think differently.
It's like no other time in your life."
- Lausa Oleynik (meetville.com)

The Origin of My Artistic Gifts

I love to work with my hands. I have come to notice that no matter what type of work that I do, I'm always creating something with my hands. Even if I'm doing an assignment on the computer, I still have to make use of my hands. Some of the work that I've done in the past were: making tutus for little girls, event decor/planning, painting, drawing, face paint for Halloween, makeup (especially eye makeup), styling hair, polishing fingernails, home designs via computer applications, crafts with children, and meal preparations, for instance. I'm so thankful for the hands that the Creator has given me. I hope that I am able to make even more magic with them.

One line of work that I wanted to get into was massage therapy. I used to massage my family and friends when I was in college. My husband was never too fond of the idea of me giving massages to strangers, which is why I didn't get into that line of work. I do enjoy using my gift of massaging on him. There are so many health benefits behind massage therapy. Massage therapy helps significantly with anxiety. It also helps with food digestion. Headaches can be relieved by getting a massage. I personally have dealt with insomnia due to stress and receiving massages regularly helps with it. Perhaps, if my husband ever changes his mind about the idea, I'll be able to get into the field of massage therapy.

"In every day, there are 1,440 minutes. That means we have 1,440 daily opportunities to make a positive impact." - Les Brown

"A steady drip of water
wears a hole in a rock."

When I heard these words said by the Colonel on the television show "A Different World", it was as if it struck me like lightening. During my lifetime, I learned the meaning of being patient and having patience. It pertained particularly to something that I had to learn especially during my youth. Some people look at me as being the most patient person that they've ever met. I would tell them that it wasn't natural for me. I had to learn it not because I wanted to, but because I had to. There weren't many things or opportunities that were given to me. It took a lot of personal sacrifices, such as being lonely throughout my life journey and being without things that a lot of people around me had. I wasn't the type to get manicures or pedicures on a regular basis. I didn't wear the popular brand names of clothing or shoes. I didn't have that "picket fence" lifestyle. I literally had to work...and work my ass off for most of the things that I have.

One day as I was driving home from a business meeting, I began to cry. My tears were heavy and draining as if I had a faucet of tears running down my face. I was overwhelmed with joy. I was overwhelmed that I had lived through so much hurt and was still standing. I was still standing to continue to make business moves. I was once told that I was nothing and will never be nothing. So to keep moving after hearing that, I felt like one of the strongest people in the world. I sat in my car that was parked in my driveway and I just let the tears pour. I was also told that crying was a form of healing. In that moment, I knew that I was healing myself even more, so I just let them come down like a waterfall. I was so thankful to the Creator for still letting me be able to stand. I felt more powerful in that moment than any time of my life. I didn't feel weakened at all. From an outside perspective, if someone saw me in my car crying the way that I was, they would have probably thought that I was hurt or sad. I was most certainly the complete opposite. I was filled with so much joy.

There is so much irony when it comes to crying. Tears can come from hurt and it can come from happiness. In that moment, my life was connected. There was a connection from my hurt and pain to my joy and happiness. I'm thankful that I was able to embrace the ties. I felt that I had finally reached my mountain top in my life.

"If I had to do it all again, I wouldn't take away the rain because it made me who I am."-Faith Evans

"If at first you don't succeed...
pick yourself up and try again."

When I was in high school, I signed up for a mock talent show. One of my favorite passions has been dancing. I like almost all forms of dance. At the initial time of hearing about the event, I had no idea as to what song I would perform or even how my dance routine would look. All I knew was that I wanted to be a part of the show. I also knew that I wanted to do a solo act. There were many talent shows and performances that I had done with a group of girls, but this time I wanted to challenge myself and do a solo act. During that time in my life, I was a huge fan of the singer Aaliyah. I liked the lyrics to a lot of her songs. More than anything, I liked the way she danced in her music videos. I noticed that she had her own style. She didn't look like a lot of the other artists in the music industry. I respected her craft and art because she was original. I like that most about people. She appeared to be within herself...she held her own.

Aaliyah was the first artist to pop in my mind when it came to who I wanted to "mock" for my performance. She had a song called "Try Again" that I really liked. I more so liked the lyrics to the song. It had a nice upbeat tempo that I was able to dance to as well. I knew that the audience would love the song. After signing up to perform the song, I was selected to be a part of the show. I knew that I was going to put my all into the performance. At the time, I had a similar hairstyle to hers. I had some of the same facial features. I knew that I could pull off the dance moves that they did in the music video. I had experience performing in front of hundreds of people, so I wasn't nervous about it. When it came time to perform, the moment that the song played, the audience went wild. There were so many Aaliyah fans. I received so many standing ovations and compliments about my performance. Still to this day, people tell me that they think of me performing her song when they hear it come on. I'm glad that I was able to celebrate Aaliyah in that light.

Besides, the performance, the lyrics to the song "Try Again" always stuck with me. It is a song of encouragement and motivation. "If at first you don't succeed...pick yourself up and try again. You can dust it off and try again..." are some of the lyrics to the song. It was a message for us to continue to move forward even if we didn't get it right the first time. That's what I love so much about life...so often we get more than one chance to succeed in life. Some of us are even able to succeed in multiple things in life. We have to give ourselves constant reminders that sometimes things won't go as we would like them to go, but we have to keep moving forward and remember to pick ourselves up and try again.

"If you promised yourself the same promise for several years and never stuck with that promise...promise yourself again, but actually stick with that promise this time around." - Toni Rain

Keep Your Femininity Inside and
Outside of The Bedroom

What you did to get him is what you need to do to keep him. I've always been a frugal spender. I don't believe in spending outrageous amounts of money on clothes. Every now and then I'll spend a pretty penny on clothes, but it's not often. But...I do believe in purchasing quality undergarments. I enjoy watching black and white films primarily from the 40's-70's. I feel that during those eras, women put more energy into their femininity. I love going to the bed in elegant attire. I also like sexy feminine undergarments. I've never been the type of woman to wear rugged t-shirts to bed. Even during the days when I was a single woman, I still made sure that I had beautiful undergarments and nice elegant sleepwear.

Oftentimes, women will wear sexy lingerie when they first become intimate with a partner. Once the two become comfortable with one another, things start to shift and the sexy lingerie stops. I never understood why so many people do that. My grandmothers used to always say, "What you did to get him is what you need to do to keep him." It stayed with me. I think that is one of the reasons why I never had a problem with guys wanting to be in long-term relationships with me. I always made sure that I kept my femininity and womanhood as a priority. I love being a woman and putting energy into myself. I also make sure that I put time into keeping up with my hygiene, especially at night. "If you stay ready, you don't have to get ready", which for me means to keep myself clean if intimacy would go into play.

I believe that you feel how you look. If I look amazing going to bed, then I feel that I'll have a more peaceful night's rest. If I put time and energy into looking great stepping out of the house, then I feel that my day will be amazing. One of my biggest pet peeves is women coming out of the house in pajamas. I've heard many women say that they don't have the time or energy to get "dressed up". I never understood that concept. My reason being is that there should always be time put into self. Self should always be a priority. When caring for others, self should be included as one to tend to as well.

"A woman who embraces her femininity
is a woman who knows her power"
- Kelly McNelis

Attacked by a Pit Bull

I was in middle school, eighth grade to be exact. It was late afternoon. My fellow school mates, family, and I were getting off the school bus, about to head home. Some of my friends' family members approached us as we were getting off the bus. As they were approaching us, I noticed that one of them was walking their tiger-striped Pit Bull. Even though I noticed the dog, I didn't have any fear. I was used to being around dogs and I've seen the dog around a few times. One of the kids in the group seemed to be a little shaken up about the dog being around. They got nervous and maneuvered their way around me and nudged me in front of them a bit. My guess is that the dog was nervous from the movement or sensed their fear. I heard a few yells. The next thing I know, the dog caught a grip of my leg. I thought that the dog was just caught in the lower half of my pant leg. I was wearing fitted cream colored jeans. I started to kick my leg, hoping that the dog would let loose of my leg but it had its mouth locked. I then started to notice blood coming through the pants. That's when I got nervous. I think that I went into shock because I couldn't feel anything.

We were on a main street, which was intersected to another main street. There were so many people outside. I could see many cars through my peripheral vision. Also, many were blowing their horns trying to get others attention. My thought is that the people in their cars were just as scared to help. The children around me were also too scared to help. I could just hear them yelling from a distance at the dog to stop. I could feel myself getting tired trying to jerk the dog from off of me. My heart began to pound harder because I was losing my strength. The owners of the dogs began to hit the dog to let me loose. I then noticed a few men that approached me. They began to kick the dog on its side and started to punch it on the top of its nose. Eventually, it let go of me. I was rushed to the hospital. At the time that I was being transported to the hospital, I still was in shock and didn't feel any pain. My pants were still held together for the most part, so I couldn't really see the damage. The doctor had to use surgical scissors to cut the pants to access the wounds on my leg. Once the pants were cut, that's when I sort of went into a panic. I could see the tissue in my legs due to the open wounds. I had three puncture wounds in my leg. They were all in my lower leg and calve muscle. I had to have tissue cut out of my leg and they had to do some draining so that I wouldn't get an infection. I was just thankful that they were able to save the leg. The family of the dog felt so bad. I didn't press charges on them because I knew that it was an accident. I actually still keep in contact with some of them. They're beautiful people.

"Relationships don't thrive because the guilty are punished but because the wounded are merciful." - Max Lucado

Used to Living a Life of Chaos

I woke up early one morning. For some reason I wasn't able to sleep throughout the night. There was nothing in particular that I could think of that was causing me to not to be fully at rest. I kept tossing and turning in my bed. I was continuously moving around, trying to adjust my body in a comfortable position. I was going back and forth with putting the sheet and comforter on and taking it off, moving it to the left side of my body. No matter what, I just couldn't get comfortable. I didn't even have to go into work that day. The night before, I was planning to sleep in a bit longer the next day so that I could recharge. I told myself that whenever a person was restless and couldn't sleep, that was the Creator telling them to get prepared for something to happen, whether good or bad. With me not being able to sleep in, I decided I'd do some yoga and get some things done around the house.

I went into another room of the house, got out my yoga mat, and did one of my hour-long yoga routines. After that, I sorted out some dirty laundry and began to wash and dry my loads of laundry. Once the laundry was washed, dried, and folded, I began to do some life reflecting. The first thing that I noticed was how peaceful and quiet it was around the house. I also realized that even outside my home, in regards to my family and close friends, that it was peaceful and quiet. It all seemed strange to me. Typically, it would seem like it would be a good thing for me instead of strange. In that moment when I realized how peaceful and quiet it was around me, I knew that I wasn't used to this. In that moment, I realized that I was used to things and people being out of order. I was used to people consistently coming to me with stress, anxiety, worries, financial issues, etc. It was unfortunate that I was expecting everything to be anything but peaceful and quiet. In that moment, I realized that I was used to things and people around me being in chaos in some way or form. I didn't find it to be normal, but strange that things were the way that they were.

I had to take a mental step back because I was thinking that way. I had to question and analyze the situation. I wanted to know if living a life of chaos was normal. I wanted to know if living a life of peace and quiet was normal. In my mind, living a life of peace and quiet was strange. I wanted to fix that. I wanted to do something about that. I wanted to live in this strange and unfamiliar space. I wanted to test it out. I wanted more of it. I wanted to smell, taste, hear, and feel more of this "strange" space that I was in. I wondered if others were living in this same unfamiliar space that I had just discovered. I wanted to know how long it would last for me. I didn't know if others noticed this new space that I was in or if it was only me seeing this reflection of myself. Either way, I didn't really care if others noticed this new space that I was in or not. I was in a selfish moment of reflection. My main focus was to get familiar with it. I wanted to get up close and personal with it. I didn't know whether I wanted to go back to my world of chaos or if I wanted to stay in this strange unfamiliar place. It was another adventure for me.

"One must still have chaos in oneself to be able to give birth to a dancing star." - Friedrich Nietzche

Losing My Uncle on My Birthday

It was a beautiful August morning. I was greeted with many birthday wishes and songs from family and friends. Even though it was pretty outside, I was filled with sadness inside. Typically, one would be filled with joy on their birthday, but I wasn't. I couldn't pinpoint where the sadness was coming from, but it was there. There was a guy that I was dating at the time, who kept asking me what I wanted for my birthday and what I wanted to do that day. I told him that I wasn't really in the mood to celebrate. Some of my friends also wanted to hang out with me that day. It took me until later that evening to make a decision to go out and try to have some fun. Even though it wasn't in my heart to do so, I went ahead and met up with some of my friends.

Before we headed out on the town to go dancing, we decided to stop at a local grocery and retail store to pick up some items. I remember having this gut feeling that something was terribly wrong. I still didn't know what it was or what was causing me to feel this sadness and emptiness in my heart. All while growing up, I was very intuitive about things that would come about. Some consider me to be an "Indigo child", meaning that I possess supernatural traits and abilities to feel and see things. I've always been able to feel other's emotions and sense things that would happen before they actually happened. While at the store, my friends and I headed to checkout to pay for the items that we were to purchase. As I was walking to check out, I looked at all the different candies and gum near the checkout counter. I picked out some of my favorite gum to purchase. Just before I was to make my purchase, something inside told me to check my phone. I looked down at it, and I was receiving an incoming call from one of my family members. My stomach dropped. I knew that it wasn't a birthday greeting. I just knew it deep down in my soul. As I answered the phone, that's when I received the news about my uncle. I remember my family member on the other side of the line saying, "Did you hear what I said?!" I was stuck. I couldn't say anything. All the while, my friends were standing beside me and looking at me while I was on the phone. The tears started to fall from my eyes. As I cried, still no words had come from my mouth. My friends just began to hold me and ask if things were alright. I finally told my family member, "Thanks for letting me know and I'll have to call you back later." From my peripheral vision, I could see and hear many people chatting amongst themselves. I even noticed others staring our way to see what was going on. The tears started to get heavier as well as my breathing. The heavy breathing then turned to heavy sounds of somber and cries. My friends asked what was wrong while they comforted me with shoulder hugs. I was trying to tell them that the phone call was about my uncle passing, but the words could hardly come out. We began to walk away from the line to head out to our vehicle. They decided that we should head back to my place. Once I was able to get my breathing and cries under control, I told them the news. I could see the sadness in their eyes for me.

I had a strong relationship with my uncle. He was always around. I even used to comb his hair. He had long hair most of his life. There were also periods of times where he would stay at our house while growing up. He had a sense of humor out of this world. There was always a joke to be told when it came to him. He was certainly a jokester in our family. In all the years that he was around, I rarely saw him upset. He was filled with laughter and with a beautiful smile to match it. After his death, it was extremely hard for me to celebrate my birthday with many people around. For years after his death, I had to go to places that was surrounded by water. Areas where there were beaches, lakes, and rivers were a comfort for me. It helped take my mind off the fact that my birthday was a reminder of my uncle's passing. It wasn't until a few years ago that I wanted to celebrate my birthday with others. I have to remind myself that my uncle was not a man of sorrow. He was a man of positive energy and happiness. He would be disappointed in the fact of me not wanting to celebrate myself. I had to look at my birthday as a celebration and a gift, again, for him. He will always be remembered for his loving and humorous spirit.

"Crying is a way your eyes speak when your mouth can't explain how broken your heart is." – Author Unknown

Finding A Love for Gardening

A few times I asked people if they could teach me how to garden. I was always told that they would help me, but I would never get a follow up. I decided that I would find a gardening program that would help me at least learn the basics of how to be a gardener. I did just that and signed up for a local program. I was able to get the knowledge that I needed and then some.

My first year of gardening was a success. I had very few problems with pests. More than anything, I was able to grow healthy fruits and vegetables organically. I didn't use any pesticides. I did everything as natural as possible. I wanted to learn how to garden even as child, but I didn't have anyone to teach me. I knew the importance of healthy eating. I read about the benefits on consuming healthy foods. Eating foods that are good for the body can help physically, emotionally, mentally, and spiritually. I also learned that a lot of the foods that I was growing has high water content and are high in antioxidants, which are natural toxic cleansers.

Outside of the foods being healthy, I love the environment of gardens. It just feels like love being in a garden. I could feel the life of the plants and the fruits by being in a garden. It puts me in a state of tranquility and peace being outdoors. It allows me to just be still for a moment. It allows me to collect my thoughts and just be in the moment. I struggle with being in the moment due to my fast-paced lifestyle. I also talk to my plants in my garden. I play music for my garden after reading about different studies being done with people playing music for plants and flowers. In some of the studies, it showed that the plants and flowers that had music played for them grew more and were healthier. I have a passion for music and know how it puts me in a peaceful state, so I figured it would do the same for the plants in my garden. I eventually want to have a farm; I've always wanted to work on a farm. I love the outdoors, so what better way to enjoy the outdoors than on my farm?

"Don't start your day with the broken pieces of yesterday. Every day is a fresh start. Each day is a new beginning. Every morning we wake up is the first day of our new life." – Author Unknown

Being Born as an Empath

As a child, I would have so many highs and lows. I didn't know what it all meant. I could look into someone's face or look at a picture of someone, and I could see and feel what their emotions were; my body just picked up on them. When I felt their emotions, it would drain me at times. Many times, a person could display a straight face, but if I looked at them, I could see tears falling from their eyes mentally. I literally could feel and see their hurt. I didn't tell my mother about it until I became an adult. I didn't want to tell her because I didn't want to be looked at as strange, weird, or crazy.

Even in my sleep I could feel people's emotions. I lost a lot of sleep because of it. Some days I would wake up out of my sleep thinking that I was dreaming what a person was going through, and then that same day or days later, I would find it to be true. I thought that if I would have told these things to my family, that I would be institutionalized. As I got older, I became more open with asking people about their feelings. I knew when I was being lied to. If a person appeared to be happy or joyful on the outside, but filled with pain and misery on the inside, I would confront them. I would ask them how they were doing. They would put on a front and then I would tell them how they were actually feeling. They would ask me how did I know what was actually going on with them. I would tell them that I could see it and feel it. They would look so puzzled. Many times, they would break down in tears. I would comfort them and let them know that I was there for them.

I rarely did this with men. I would comfort women primarily. Growing up I was looked at as the "cool kid" by many, but to a lot of people I was still looked at as weird. I didn't dress like many people in my neighborhood. I oftentimes wore bows, flowers, and ribbon in my hair to stand out. I was also told that I dressed like an old woman because of my vintage flare. As a child, no one wanted to be looked at as weird. Now, I embrace being called weird because I look at it as a sign of being unique and standing out.

"Today will never come again. Be a blessing. Be a friend. Encourage someone. Take time to care. Let your words heal, and not wound." – Author Unknown

Marriage: Business Venture or Sign of Pure Bliss?

Almost everywhere you look, there is marriage. It's pretty much embedded in a little girl to get married at the toddler stages of life. Growing up, I watched all of the animated movies and cartoons which portrayed young women falling in love over "Prince Charming". In fact, marriage does not portray those fairytales at all in my eyes. There are definitely moments of love, but marriage is not always a romantic scene. There are scenes of hurt, stress, frustration, infidelity, and other mishaps. Marriage is work...a lot of work. You have to work harder at it than anything that you've ever worked hard at in your life.

Some married people say that it should be a priority and #1 in your life. I agree to a certain extent. I put my marriage first if I feel that my husband puts me first in his life. I feel that if I looked at marriage only for the love portion of it, I don't think that I would have stayed in my marriage. I have had to look at marriage from different avenues in order for me to understand it. I realized that people's views of marriage all varied. No one marriage is like any other. Marriage is what you make it. At least, that's what I've learned over the years.

I've seen many broken marriages. I've seen only a few "successful" marriages. More than anything, I see marriage as a business. I say marriage is a business, because for one, a marriage license is a contract between two or more parties. Once you get married, you can even get tax benefits. There are many different "breaks" that a person gets, whether male or female, once you are married. If you purchase a home or other entity while married and things don't work out, you can't just walk away from those responsibilities. You both sign and co-sign for those properties— making a business decision for those properties.

I've gotten some backlash for saying that a marriage should not just be looked at from just a love and affection standpoint, but also from a business standpoint. For my husband and I, almost every decision is made together when it comes to our property and the way that things are handled in our home. On another note, others will try to tell you and your spouse how to run your marriage. That's just like someone walking into a business and telling the owner/owners how they should be running their business. Like the old saying goes, "Don't let too many hands stir the pot." I learned that for myself at a young age, thankfully. I've never been the type of person to let others control my life. I appreciate others opinions and words of wisdom, but when it comes to making life choices and decisions, I take my own advice.

I have also learned that people will tell you not to do something that they would do. Over the years, I realized how hypocritical a lot of people can be. In fact, some will tell you not to do or put up with something that they would put up with 10 or more times over. Your mind and your heart will lead you to making positive decisions and choices more often than individuals will. My advice is to take your own advice. There are keys that I have told myself about marriage. Here are 10 that I've come up with in regards to marriage:

1) Design your marriage in your own way (no marriages are the same).

2) You don't have to live a "traditional marriage" (Don't put roles or labels on what you and your husband should/shouldn't do).

3) Be your spouse's friend.

4) Whatever you can do with your girlfriends/sisters/girls/or fellow Queens, you should be able to do with your spouse.

5) Don't always take advice from others. Sometimes they will put up with 10 times worse than what they are telling you not to put up with.

6) If tension is too high between you and your spouse, write letters or notes to each other to express how you feel.

7) Set a date night for the two of you each week and stick to it.

8) Love on each other as much as possible.

9) It's okay to go out on a "self-date" from time to time to give each other space and time to miss one another.

10) You don't have to make family/ friends inclusive in your marriage if you feel disrespected by them.

"Coming together is a beginning; keeping together is a progress; working together is success"- Henry Ford

Speak Life into The Things You Want

Ask the Universe for the things that you want. I'm a firm believer of speaking life into the things that you want. There's the old saying, "Ask and you shall receive." I used to pout to myself all the time when I was a child. I'd shut myself off from the world, or so I thought. I was notorious for closing my bedroom door as a child to shut everyone out when I was overwhelmed, frustrated, or angry. I thought that I instantly became invisible to everyone by shutting my door. It was my way of saying, "Leave me alone!" Most times when I separated myself from everyone, it was because I really wanted something that either I or the family needed. To the common person, when someone is pouting, it seems as though a person is bratty or spoiled. In fact, I did want to be spoiled in a sense; I wasn't interested in being spoiled with luxury but with things of necessity. The things of necessities that I often wanted were consistency of running water, heat/hot water, electricity, or other utilities.

Many times, it was a struggle for my mother to keep up with the utility bills. As a child, you don't really understand the concept of life. As a child you don't fully understand the sacrifices that go along with life. You don't understand that sometimes when an adult goes to work, that doesn't necessarily mean that the money that they make from working that job will cover all the bills. As a young person, you don't understand that sometimes the parent or guardian has to choose between having sufficient funds to only cover one or two of the utilities and providing food. Sometimes they have to decide whether to cover any of the utility bills when only really being able to pay for food. As a child, you don't quite know what the meaning of getting an eviction notice is and having so much time to gather your belongings and getting out of your place of residence. Even with getting that eviction notice, as a child you don't know that once you're out of that place of residence that you then have to move to another unknown residence. So, in while a child is trying to understand this, they're not knowing that their parent or guardian has so many thoughts of how they're going to piece everything together for the child or children. So many times, I would get excited when my mother would bring home a paycheck, only to get another heartache or internal breakdown because she'd say, "Yes I just got paid, but I'm still broke, so I won't be able to pay for anything extra." I didn't understand it then. How can someone get paid and still be broke at the same time? It didn't make sense to me that the woman who was our provider and protector who worked to pay the bills didn't have enough money to pay the bills. As a child, you don't understand how hard it could be for a single mother of four to struggle so much, all while working. Also, on top of taking care of us, she was also helping with taking care of other family members, friends, and neighborhood children as well. There were so many children that she took in, as well as adults, that I lost count. Looking back now, I don't know how she was able to help so many people when she was struggling with helping herself and the four children that she had to raise. Some people see me now and they have no idea of what kind of childhood I had. As the great Langston Hughes said, "Life for me ain't been no crystal stair."

Mother to Son
By: Langston Hughes
Well, son, I'll tell you. Life for me ain't been no crystal stair. It's had tacks in it, And splinters, And boards torn up, And places with no carpet on the floor — Bare. But all the time I'se been a-climbin' on. And reachin' landin's.
And turnin' corners, And sometimes goin' in the dark Where there ain't been no light. So boy, don't you turn back. Don't you set down on the steps 'Cause you finds it's kinder hard. Don't you fall now— For I'se still going, honey, I'se still climbing, And life for me ain't been no crystal stair (From Collected Poems).

There was some help in regards to additional income for our household. We received government assistance. Growing up it was looked at as an embarrassment to receive government assistance rather than as a gift or a blessing. Little did I know that there were other people who I grew up with getting assistance as well. There were also family members and my mother's friends who have helped on occasions when or if they could. Sometimes I wonder if we didn't have the help if we'd be living on the streets. It took me years, after just sitting in my room pouting over things that I had no control over, to realize that this wasn't going to solve any of the problems. I began verbally saying and crying out loud for the things my family needed. Once I became of age to work, I asked out loud that a job came along my way. Sure enough, I was able to find some babysitting jobs after school. I began working at the age of 12, continuing to work up until this present day. I've been fortunate enough to find consistent work because I've asked the Creator for it. I've spoken to and cried out to the Universe for steady employment. By the time I was 13, there were summer programs in my area available for teens. I worked those programs faithfully every year. I knew that I would be able to bring home money to help my family if I was able to have a job. I worked full time every summer each year up until it was time for me to go off to college. With the money that I was bringing home, I was able to contribute to the financial responsibilities. A few years after I was in the summer program, my brother who is the first child under me, applied for a job doing the same duties and he was accepted. The cycle continued and we were able to both bring in extra income. One of my other younger brothers joined the program when he became of age as well.

At this time during my teen years, school dances were also of interest to me. I needed money for these dances, so I found other work throughout the school year to pay for costs associated with going to the high school dances. I wanted to make my own income to cover the costs because I knew that it would be a burden on my mother to have to pay for all of those expenses. There was a guy in high school that I dated who also helped with some of the expenses. I realized that the more I opened my mouth and asked for the help that I needed, the easier life got for us. I had to put my pride aside. I've always been prideful about asking for help. I never wanted to be a burden to anyone or even to the Creator. I felt like I was always begging for something. I always felt like I needed something every day, in which I actually did need something every day. Even as a child helping with expenses, there was still money that was needed for something in the house. There were only so many hours that a child or teen could work. The pay rate wasn't as high as it would have been if we were adults.

The older that I got, I was finally starting to realize and understand my mother's words of how you can work and still be broke. I was then starting to understand the concepts of adulthood. I saw families on television with dual parenting, nice houses, the utilities appearing to work, happy faces, and nice vehicles. They seemed to have comfortable lifestyles. I was curious as to how the actors on TV were living their comfortable lifestyle. I wanted the lifestyle that they had. I was going to figure out how those families were able to receive comfort. I wanted it so bad. Oftentimes in scenes, you would see the parents coming home after a long day. I thought that maybe I had to work longer days and put in more hours of work. I did just that. I picked up extra work. I did side projects and I learned how to style hair. I styled hair for close friends and some family members for a small fee. Even when I went to college, I was styling people's hair in my dorm, their dorm rooms, and at nearby apartment complexes off campus. I also worked on the college campus each year through my bachelor's degree program. I was determined to find a way to have a better lifestyle. I was going to cry out externally and internally until I was able to live a "comfortable lifestyle".

"Don't be afraid to give yourself everything you've ever wanted."
– From powerofpositivity.com

I Believe in Having Financial Freedom

       I didn't realize the true concept of financial freedom until after college. I learned the importance of liabilities and assets. Early in life, I got myself into some financial burdens. While in college, I wanted to look nice whenever I would attend an event or went out on the town. I would literally have to have a new outfit at least once or twice a week. With me not having extra spending money in my bank account to afford all of these things, I started applying for credit cards. I didn't learn the pros and cons of having a credit card. I didn't do my research as to which ones I should and shouldn't apply for. I didn't compare and contrast the different interest rates or terms and conditions of the different credit card companies. The amounts started adding up and spiraling out of control. I didn't have anyone to hold my hand or walk me through what I should have done with getting the amounts paid down. I started doing my own research on how to get the payments down. I even tried to consolidate all of the amounts.

       Right after college, I learned more about credit card debt. The word "debt" frightened me. I also had some student loans that I had to pay off that also contributed to my debt amount. On top of these bills, I had the utilities and my rent that I had to pay. After talking to a few seasoned adults, they taught me how to get some of my payments down. I also realized that material things were not all that important anymore. Most of the things that I was purchasing had no real value. I wasn't making wise purchasing decisions at all. I learned that it was best to purchase items or make investments that would appreciate over time. I had a love for cars, but I found out that they depreciate over time and lose their value, especially if it's not a classic vehicle. I started to invest and spend my money wisely. I made sure to pay off my debt. I started changing my eating habits. I realized that eating out was a waste of so much of my money. My husband started preparing 90% of my meals to keep me from spending and wasting so much money. I started thrifting and purchasing discounted items more often when I needed clothes or items for the house or everyday way of living. I also found out about couponing, so I became an avid coupon user. There was a time when I was swamped with work that I didn't have the time to dedicate to couponing, so I connected with other coupon users. I would pay a small fee for the items that they were getting for free. I still was saving money by purchasing from other couponers, because I wasn't paying full retail value. Every avenue I was able to save money, I tried to make it a common practice.

I was tired of seeing my hard earned income going to waste. I knew that if I made more positive decisions and healthier habits of my spending that I would get further in life when it came to financial freedom. I learned that the higher a person's credit score was, the easier it would be for gaining access to loans for business ventures if needed. I wanted to save and build my credit score. I wanted my credit score to be polished so, if need be, I could borrow from investors. If I were to take out a loan, it would more so be in relation to business or entrepreneurship. I wasn't going to use it for recreational use. I also believe in borrowing from myself out of my own personal accounts, learning the benefits of borrowing from myself. I'm still prideful when it comes to borrowing money from other people, so I try to borrow money from myself first and foremost. There is a saying that says, "You have to have money to make money." I now see the meaning of those words. Having a low credit score can hinder you in so many ways. It can hinder you from purchasing a home, starting a business, or purchasing a car. For me, those things are necessities. They are part of my comfortability.

With me going through periods of not having a stable place to live, I always wanted a place to call home. I've always wanted to be a homeowner. Once my credit was cleaned up and a lot of my debt was paid off, my husband and I purchased a home. We purchased our home a few years after we both graduated from college. This was a stressful time in life, but at the same time it felt so rewarding. He had a pretty good credit score prior to us purchasing a home. I had to clean mine up right after college, and I did exactly that. I wanted that same financial freedom as he had. All while I was still trying to maintain a healthy credit score, I also wanted to have a nice stream of revenue. I've been investing in different business ventures. I've always wanted to see my name in a Fortune 500 magazine. I wanted to have a healthy stream of income; not just for me but for my extended family as well. I want there to always be opportunities for my family members to always have a place for employment. I want to be able to have multiple businesses to employ a good majority of my family, especially if they struggle to find employment. I want to be able to keep the doors of employment open to them. I continue to speak life into that idea.

"Narrow minds will become wider. But when change is in people faces, everybody goes into pain mode, everybody freaks out and starts to worry about what they would lose, and not what they would gain." - Eric Jerome Dickey

The First in My Family to Receive
a Diploma and College Degree

During my youth, I don't recall many people talking about school. I actually heard more discussion about people dropping out of school. It seemed to be a popular thing for people to skip school; it was bragged upon. Youth and teen pregnancy were also evident and another very popular topic of discussion. From watching television shows such as "A Different World", "The Cosby Show", and "Family Matters", to name a few, I realized that finishing high school and going to college was actually a good thing. It was looked at as a fun and exciting thing to do. The young people from the shows seemed as if they were looking forward to enrolling and graduating from school.

I also looked at going to college as a guaranteed source of receiving an income. Growing up as a child, having a continuous source of income was a yearly struggle. I not only saw it in my household, but in many households around me, including those of my family members and neighbors. From what I saw on TV, I looked at going to college as a means of getting out of the struggle. I also knew that selling illegal drugs and "running numbers" was also another way of gaining income. Most of the people that I knew who took this illegal route for making money oftentimes ended up going to jail and prison. I did not want that for myself. I couldn't mentally see myself taking that route or going through anything like that. I didn't know of anyone successfully selling illegal drugs or running numbers. Even from watching movies about mafias and drug cartels, I didn't see any of those people being successful in the end with their illegal activities. If people with that much movement couldn't go through that lifestyle without getting caught, I knew that people of my stature wouldn't be successful either. I only saw college as an option for myself.

I also found out that college was costly. I was told that I probably wouldn't be able to attend because I wasn't financially stable. During my high school years, I went on school and after-school trips to visit colleges and universities. I went to visit local and many out-of-state schools. Thankfully, I was eligible for grants and funding to be able to visit these schools free of charge. I went to after-school programs from the age of 12-18 faithfully. The siblings in my household all went to the same after-school programs throughout their adolescent and teenage years as well. We all learned about colleges and universities primarily from outside sources. I was so "green" whenever we would have open discussions about higher education during these programs. It seemed as if most of the other students knew far more about the different schools than I did. At times I had to center myself. I had to tell myself, *you cannot help what you don't know*. I still tell myself that at times as a reminder. I took what I did know and learn as tools. I used them as tools for preparation for my future life.

In those programs, I also learned about tests, such as the ACT and SAT, which needed to be taken prior to applying for college. I received a grant from high school which paid for the costs of taking my ACT test. Thankfully, I passed my first time taking it although I was extremely nervous. If I had failed, I was unsure of where I would get more funds to cover the cost to retake it. I had to give myself a pep talk. I told myself to not see failure as an option. I told myself that if I went into the test thinking that I would fail, then chances were that I would in fact fail. I learned about other financial resources, such as financial aid, for instance. There was another program called T.I.P. (Tuition Incentive Program) that was available for me. Only certain schools participated with this program.

I originally wanted to attend a university farther away from home, just to get a break from my surroundings and what I had always known. I then learned about out of state fees when attending college. I wanted to attend a school that would cover the majority of my costs and fees. My family was not too happy or set on me attending a college or university far away from home. The thought of being away from my family was actually petrifying for me. My family was all that I had known. I lived in one city my entire youth and adolescent years. I traveled a lot growing up, but it didn't compare to living in a city most of your life. I hear a lot of people who are from my hometown complaining about it often. Despite the troubles that I faced while being in my city, I still had unconditional love for it. I wanted to pour as much love into the city as I was able to. I knew that I had a lot of people looking up to me in my hometown. It wasn't just family watching me, but also friends and other people in the city.

I often wondered what caused people to have a lack of drive and perseverance. I didn't quite understand how someone would become complacent with not wanting to continue their education. I questioned what other factors were in the way of them even completing getting a high school diploma. I wanted to know where it stemmed from to make them want to quit. Being that I didn't allow my upbringing to keep me from pushing forward, I didn't understand how people could say that someone is a product of their environment. I don't necessarily agree with that saying. I never felt as if I was a product of my environment because I have always had my own interests and desires from most of the people that I was around. There was a spark in me to go far in life. It was in me to make my family proud. I wanted to be an example that if I can make it to the finish line, that they could do it as well.

I come from a large family. I knew that I was going to have nieces, nephews, and little cousins watching me in addition to my siblings. I graduated from elementary, middle school, and high school with honors. When it came time to go to college, I was nervous and often uncomfortable. It was hard for me to focus on my academics, because I worried about what was going on at home. Whenever I would call home, I could hear the worry in their voices, which caused me to worry for them. I decided to attend a university in a city that wasn't too far from my hometown. I didn't do so well my first year of college. I passed all of my classes, but I was no longer an honor student. That was tough for me. I was an honors student from elementary up until I graduated from high school. My sophomore year of college was probably the most mentally challenging for me. After my first year of college, I decided to go back to my hometown and attend a university there. My grades were much better than they were my freshman year of college, but I was in a mentally depressed state of mind. I had connected with a lot of people at the university that I attended during my freshman year. I also got involved in different organizations and I loved being a part of them. I was torn between being there for my family and my own educational happiness. I wanted both, but I knew that I had to decide between the two.

I also met some lifelong friends at the university in my hometown, but my experience wasn't nearly the same. The university in my city was extremely boring to me. The campus was much smaller and they did not have organizations that I was interested in joining. My family could also sense that I wasn't happy moving back home. I was also receiving more grant and scholarship money at the school in my hometown. I had to decide as to whether I was going to stay in my hometown or go back to the university that made me the happiest. I went for my happiness. I knew that if I didn't go away to a school that would bring me to a better mental state, that I wouldn't have as much drive to complete getting my college degree.

I decided that I would take as many college credits that I would be able to take at a time. I ended up completing college and receiving my bachelor's degree within a four-year time span. Some people who knew my background were quite surprised. I heard some say that I was going to end up pregnant and drop out. In all honesty, it was hearing things like this that gave me more drive to go further in my education. I applied for a managerial position a few months after graduating and I received the offer for the position. Shortly after working that job, I took more college courses. I received a certification and also took some master-level courses, but I didn't complete the master's program.

I basically ended up receiving six-years of college education. Even after those accomplishments, I still wasn't satisfied with the education that I received. One thing that stood out to me the most in regards to college is that I do not recall my professors ever mentioning that a person should try to work for themselves. I don't ever remember them focusing on entrepreneurship. When I was a little girl, I always talked about running a business and working for myself. It was never really a thought for me to want to work for someone else. I didn't like the fact that most of the time there was a cap amount on how much salary you would make while working a job. That didn't set well with me. I wanted to decide how much money I wanted to make for myself. I never liked putting limits or "caps" on anything in my life. I was never comfortable with that thought.

"The closer one gets to realizing his personal legend, the more that personal legend becomes his true reason for being." - The Alchemist

What Sets Me Apart?

I've always caused the ripples in my waves. If they try to box me in, I chip and thump through their corners. My agenda may change several times, so most times it's never truly set. I realize that I don't have a favorite color. I like them all. I'm an Indigo and I embrace it more as the years go by. That is I. I love to love and I'm certainly not shameful for it. It's much easier to smile than to make a frown. Being angry and upset with the world will leave me with a heart full of holes like a pumice stone. I'd rather have most of my holes filled with as much love that can possibly fill them. The only way to fill those holes is to put out the love that I do have left and hopefully the universe will bring that same love back to me. I'd never give up on life because life never gave up on me. When I was bruised, those wombs were able to heal. No, I was never the same, but the body naturally heals itself...not completely, but it still does heal. Once you grasp on to pain and recognize it, it becomes easier to let it heal. The problem with people who aren't able to let go of pain is that most times they can't learn to accept that it was just a period of their life that happened by design. There are things that will come about in a person's life that is out of their control. We don't and can't control everything that has happened or will happen in our lives. As much as we would like to control things in our life, sometimes we just can't. That's where our life's navigation comes into play. We have to mentally, more than physically, navigate through our life.

"Be somebody who makes everybody feel like a somebody."
–Author Unknown

Intertwining Love, Life, and Peace into My Daily Life
(if it's not there, then find it!)

A close friend of mine asked me, "Do you suffer from depression? Do you have any mental disabilities?" I was shocked at the questions. I didn't know if it was coming from concern or sarcasm. I looked into their eyes, and I saw only a question of concern. They continued: "Well...you've experienced a lot of trauma in your life, more than the average person. It would seem like you would suffer from depression." I stalled with my response for a few seconds. My response was that I didn't think that I was depressed, but on the inside, my body was saying something else. *Why are you lying like that?! Yes, you are. You know that you are. You are just trying to hide it.* I wasn't going to tell them about my crying spells. I wasn't going to tell them about the many nights that I would wake up from having nightmares. I wasn't going to tell them about my emotional and physical pain. I wasn't going to tell them that I used sex as a mechanism to relieve stress and mental hurt. No, I wasn't going to tell them any of those things. Deep inside they knew that there was something wrong. They didn't verbally respond by telling me that I was lying to them. Their eyes did though. They began to help me.

One day I was asked, "Do you like tea?" I told them that I wasn't really a fan of it. They explained the benefits of it and how it relieved people. They suggested that I start to drink tea. I was also asked if I was a fan of the water. I told them that I loved being surrounded by water. I was always intrigued by rivers, lakes, and oceans. Any chance that I was able to, I wanted to be near water. I am a woman of nature. My most peaceful moments have been spent outdoors. I was then asked to go for a walk by the river. After months had gone by, I realized that drinking tea and visiting the river became a regular event for us. We would sit and talk about life. I laughed until my stomach began to hurt. It didn't take long to realize that they were one of my biggest support systems. In those months, it was one of the darkest moments in my life. I had gone through so much over the years that eventually things had begun to catch up with me mentally. In those moments of having "tea time" and going to the river, it made things so much brighter for me. I was able to get lost in the moments. It was a natural healing for me in those moments of sipping tea and watching the waves. I wonder if they knew the severity of my hurt. I think they had a glimpse, but I don't think that they knew the depths of it. All I knew was that they were sent to be by my side. I remember telling them that they were my Earth Angel. I'm unsure if they took me serious or not, but I deemed it as true.

My family and friends are supportive when they can be. Most of them have families to tend to, so it would be selfish of me to invade them with the personal issues that I had going on. Most times when I would have breakdowns or crying spells, I'd be alone. I never like for people to see me cry. Most people see me as "the strong one". I realized many years ago that the "strong ones" need to be saved and helped at times also. With most of my inner circle being busy with their own personal lives, I often felt alone during those darkest moments in my life. My Earth Angel could see this. They knew what natural remedies I needed. I was always against prescription drugs. I wasn't going to take a pill to help me cope with it. I knew that I needed self-healing. It felt good to have someone in my corner. It felt good to have a shoulder to lean against. It felt good to have someone to talk to, call, or even just send or receive a text message from. It felt good to not be a burden, a victim, or a "cry for help." It felt good just to be loved, even from being wounded from the inside and out. I looked at it as being able to be loved, even when most parts of me inside were dead. I felt as if most of my soul had died. The little bit that I had left was barely holding on. As to what it was holding on to, I was unsure. Many times I reflected on what my family and friends would think if I were to just give up; giving up on hope, drive, ambition, love, or even all of these things. My Earth Angel saw that I had fight left in me. They didn't want me to give up. I looked back on them sending me a message saying, "You're just sooooo lucky to be loved and needed in so many peoples' lives. Great leaders have killed for that kind of love and affection." They also used to compare me to the moon. They always said that I stood out outside from the stars. In those precious moments, I felt precious for once. I felt delicate and loved. I knew that in those moments, it was ok to embrace who I was. They were tender reminders that people do really love and look up to me. It was up to me to find that same love and light in me that everyone else saw. People put the thought in my mind, so I was going to go on that journey of finding it also.

There were moments in my life where I actually embraced life. I love to make people laugh and smile as much as I can. Seeing others happy reflect back to me and make me happy as well. I began to sit on that idea in my mind. I knew that the more I loved on others, the more that I was loving on myself. My love for them brought more self-love to me. I asked myself one day, *Why is it so hard for me to love me, the way that I love others? Why am I putting myself last in the equations oftentimes more than less?* I had some serious love making that needed to happen...self-love. Once it clicked into my mind that I needed more self-healing, life became much easier to endure. I've always heard people say, "You have to love on you first, before you can love someone else." It seemed as if this saying was true, but I had to actually apply it. Eventually, I did start to apply it. Once I started to move into this transition, I started seeing other changes around me. I started to see a disconnect between quite a few people. I would sometimes hear, "Where have you disappeared to?" or "You fell off the face of the earth!", when in fact, I didn't disappear or fall off from them. What I had done prior was disappear from loving on myself. I had fallen off on loving on myself. Others were so used to me doing and catering to others, that it looked unusual for them to see me actually spending more time with myself. I sometimes surprised myself with how much love that I started to pour into myself. It got to the point that I actually didn't feel humane when I wasn't giving myself time. I would not feel comfortable in my skin if I didn't make daily quiet time or self-care time. One thing that I found myself doing to keep my peace within myself was to date myself. I wouldn't wait to go places with others, such as the movies, breakfast, lunch, dinner, etc. If I wanted to go somewhere nice and spare of the moment, I did just that, even if alone. I didn't or don't have to wait on others to do everything with me. I became comfortable and confident doing things solo. It was all a part of loving on me and finding that peace within me. Also, I wasn't being a distraction to others' daily routine or them having to alter their plans if I wanted to do something spare of the moment.

"A meaningful life is not being rich, being popular, being highly educated, or being perfect. It is about being real, being humble, being strong, and being able to show ourselves, and touch the lives of others. It is only then that we could have a full, happy, and contented life." – Author Unknown

Starting an "Accidental Business"

Shortly after I graduated from college, I started to have severe dry skin and scalp issues. I thought that it could have been hormonal. I actually never had problems with my skin growing up. I had a few acne pimples here and there, but never problems in regards to dry skin. I tried different over-the-counter creams. I even went to see a dermatologist about my skin issues. The creams and prescriptions didn't work for me. What I tried only made my condition worse. I decided to take a more natural approach. I went to natural goods stores and businesses around the neighborhood. I liked the products that were sold and some worked for me to help with my skin and scalp condition. There was one issue that I had when it came to purchasing some of the products. The costs were high for my budget. Also, I realized that I had to purchase different products for different areas of my body. I decided to do my own research on what medicinal ingredients were good for healing my body. I went and purchased some of the ingredients. I mixed the different ingredients together and started making creams and sprays for myself. My husband and I started using the products. There was such a significant difference in our skin, scalp, and hair texture. I no longer had problems with scalp dandruff or rough skin patches. My husband would often get compliments about how his skin looked like it was glowing. Both of us also had dramatic hair growth. We were both using products on all parts of our body, including using the same product for our hair and scalp.

I also had some issues with arthritis and body aches. My husband would rub the creams into my skin while giving me massages. There was so much relief in my joints after he used the products on me. I soon realized that the creams that I made at my home were multi-usage. They could all be used for the hair, body, and for massages. I also made multi-use body mists. We used the mists for our hair and also as an after bath/shower mist for added moisture. Occasionally, people would ask me what products I was using for myself that had my hair growing and my skin glowing. I told them that I was making products at home. Close friends and relatives began to ask if they could purchase the products I was making. In the beginning, I was giving out large amounts of the creams and bottles of the mist. One person asked me, "Why are you giving away your amazing products? You do realize this is a business right? You should be charging people for your time, your services, and your products. You are investing a lot of your personal time and gifts. You should be getting paid for it."

It took for someone else to tell me that I actually had a business. Since I was a child in elementary, I always knew that I wanted to have a business. As a child, I didn't really know what a business was, but I did know that I wanted to make things and do things on my own. Even then as a child, I liked to find projects to raise my own money. All my life, I was a great dancer. I used to love to perform for my family and some of my family's friends. Sometimes I wouldn't want to perform when asked. I remember one of my family members saying that they would pay me if I performed a dance for them. A light bulb went off (figuratively speaking). I took advantage of performing after that. Most times I would charge a small fee for them to see me perform. I had an entrepreneurial mindset at a very young age. Also, as a child, I used to have my family come get me or have me come over to their home if they needed cleaning work done for a small fee. I knew how to clean an entire kitchen including sweeping and mopping while I was in kindergarten. I also knew how to wash and wring out clothes by hand. I would sometimes even charge to do store runs for them. I was pretty much working for myself at a young age. These were all building blocks for my adulthood; I just didn't realize it until my adult years.

Hard work and perseverance have all helped me to this day. It also helped me build a foundation and consideration for customer service. I always wanted to do a good job when performing or doing a service for someone. I wanted to persevere in all areas of my life. I always wanted to leave them with good energy and a smile. I love making people feel good. It's much easier to make someone happy than to make someone sad. When it comes to me making my products, I was also making people feel good. I was helping them feel better about their skin, scalp, and body pain. I was helping them feel more relaxed when they received their massages or were giving themselves massages.

"Always make major moves when you're not moving and even when you're silent. The mind should always forever be widening. Work even when you're working." - Toni Rain

Who Just Wants to Live an Unfulfilling Life?

Most of my life, I wanted to be of help to someone. Even those that I just meet, I try to leave them with some sort of life key, words of wisdom, or some kind of positive vibe. Not everything that you give to someone has to be tangible or have some type of financial value. Receiving positive feedback can be useful most times. You may not need it at the moment when it's given or received, but it can be resourceful later on in life. Those words can be used as building blocks for something bigger later on down in your life. Growing up, I was surrounded by people much older and wiser than myself. They were always giving me words of wisdom. They used to say, "You may not want to hear it now, but you will need it when you're older." They were absolutely right about that. A lot of things that were said when I was much younger didn't click in my head until I was in my adulthood.

My recommendation for the children of today is to pay attention to adults when they give you words of wisdom, because, more than likely, you'll need that valuable information. Sometimes I look back and think where my life would be had I not listened. I've done some pretty risky things in my life, but the words from the wise and mature would often times pop in my head when I would want to take some risks that weren't worth taking. Through it all, I still made sure that I handled and took care of my priorities. No matter what, business and home responsibilities always came first. The times when I wanted to go out on the town, take a trip somewhere, or just sit around and do absolutely nothing at times, I made sure that my responsibilities were taken care of first. Those same words of advice that were told to me, I am now able to pass them down to the younger generation. Adults can always use words of wisdom about things that they don't know as well.

I feel that my life is being fulfilled by being able to help and teach people things that can help them throughout their lives. I've done various things in my life and I have an extensive work history. I've helped people write resumes. I've done mock interviews with people to help them find employment. Many people have used me as a reference for them to gain employment. I worked for a home improvement company in a managerial position, so I've helped people build their homes, designed kitchen and deck layouts, and assisted in other areas of home improvement. I've been resourceful in helping others build their dream homes. I've worked with children, so I was able to help families be able to talk to their children. Sometimes parents get frustrated with kids, but I've learned how to deal and work with children to where problems would be able to be resolved. I've always worked well with children and I'm so thankful for that. With foods being genetically modified at a higher level, I learned to grow healthy organic food as well. I love to eat food. I primarily love to eat healthy food.

When I was in college, I did an interview with my maternal grandfather about his upbringing. One of the things that stood out the most about the interview session is that he mentioned how people should get back to doing more farming and more gardening. I did this interview with him as a part of an assignment for one of my college courses. Prior to doing the assignment, I didn't realize how important having a farm or a garden was. My grandfather told me how much healthier and more tasteful their food was growing up because they grew most of their own food. He taught me the importance of eating fresh foods over eating fast food or processed food. He is no longer with us, but his words will last with me forever. Thankfully I listened. I made sure that when I shopped for foods while in college, that I selected the healthier foods. On the weekends, I would sometimes visit different farmers markets. Some of my friends had gardens and they would grow different fruits and vegetables for me as well. Some years after purchasing my home, I decided to take some gardening courses. I too learned how to grow some of my own foods. The words of my grandfather traveled with me throughout my life. I wanted to grow healthy organic food, not just for myself, but also for my family and friends. We have to realize that we take a lot of the necessities that we have for granted. Remember that there are people who don't have the adequate resources that some of us have. We fight against ourselves to eat healthier foods and those with a lack of access to it envy us. Anytime someone comes to my home, they may not see a full refrigerator but best believe that there will be fruits and veggies available. Also, when shopping for food, shop on the outside perimeters. That's where most of the foods that you actually should be eating are.

"I have found that if you love life, life will love you back."
– Arthur Robinstein

Focus on Your Priorities...Focus on You

Material things should never be put first before investments. Oh...and stay out of other folks' business and tend to your own. Your main focus should always be self first. In order to help or look out for someone else, your foundation has to be solid. Your foundation is self. Your wealth is your health. There are people who are wealthy financially with the poorest health. I'm sure the majority of those with wealth and poor health would trade in their money to have a healthy body. You also want to have a healthy mental. It's perfectly fine to cater to most of your own needs. Keep yourself in balance as much as possible. With the outside world and life being so busy, it's very easy to lose self while in it. I've lost myself a few times over my lifetime, so I know this to be true.

I see so many people valuing material things. At times, you can purchase things that you typically won't ever need or use. It can sit in your closet or sit on your shelves without ever being used or touched. I've done this many times before in my younger days. I thought about how much money I wasted looking back on those years. I quickly found out that I would never want to "keep up with the Jones". It wasn't worth it to me. Me purchasing those material things wasn't even all that important, looking back. I learned that you can have nice things without having to spend so much of your hard earned money. I also was not big into having name brand fashions. There were times where I could make a $50 wardrobe look like a $500 wardrobe, for instance. I also noticed that those who did have wealth didn't look like the stereotype of someone with wealth. The wealthy aren't always flashy people. Sometimes they can look rugged or more like "common folk". You simply can't judge someone's lifestyle by what they wear or even what kind of vehicle they drive. Instead of focusing on material things, the things that should be focused on are investments.

There are a few things that a person can invest in. Here are a few things that I would recommend: 401k plan, Roth IRAs, Savings Bonds, Mutual Funds, bank CDs, and starting a business/businesses. You should want to invest your money into things or accounts that will help your funds to grow or appreciate over time. In my case, I would rather put money towards these things instead of wasting money on things that have no real value to them. As a whole, you should want to focus on your physical health, mental health, and your financial stability. When you are your focal point, you tend to make your business your business. So often I see people getting themselves involved in other people's lives much more than they should be. Sometimes it can be overwhelming when others focus more on you than on themselves. Granted we always want others to love and show concern for us, but it should be kept to a certain level. In my case, I love to receive love and affection, but I also value my personal space physically and mentally. It took me a long time to let others know if they were being too overbearing by being in "my space". I have a problem with people who I hardly know being in my personal business. I don't like to be looked at as being nosey, so I try to give myself boundaries when it comes to being in people's space. I feel that others should have the same practices. I personally feel that a person's life would be so much more peaceful if they weren't so consumed with others personal lives. I've come to know that some people come with some heavy or intense lifestyles, so I'm unsure as to why they would want to put those worries on themselves when they have so much to worry about or tend to for themselves. Not only that, when you try to pry or be too involved or consumed with others' lives and don't set boundaries for yourself, you can cause those people that you pry on to have anxiety. I, for instance, started to have social anxiety because people were too much into my personal business and space. It made me become more withdrawn from dealing with a lot of people. For the most part, I have some family members that I hang out with on a regular basis and only a select few friends that I socialize with. The reason being is that I was bombarded by people on multiple occasions. It literally caused me to put a halt on most people.

I like to live with boundaries. It allows me to be less stressful and less anxious. Some have recognized the change. In my younger years, I always had people surrounding me. I was known in my hometown for throwing parties and events. As I got older, I realized that it wasn't the most mentally healthy thing for me. Some people don't have good intentions and don't wish you well or even want you to succeed. There are people who just simply want to be around you or be under you for their own advantage. I realize that not all people are trustworthy. I've personally had people who I was closest to steal from me or drag my name in the dirt. It caused me to be very guarded with who I have around me or even in my corner. Even with some of life's situations, it still didn't keep me from loving or caring for people. I just have some walls and guards up in certain areas of my life.

"My to do list for today: Count my blessings -practice kindness - Let go of what I can't control - Listen to my heart - Be productive yet calm - Just breathe" - Funchap

Vibrate to Your Highest Potential

When you are always vibrating high, it's almost unbearable for those who vibrate low to want to be around you. You will have to learn to be comfortable with that uncomfortable fact. You can't bring everyone to your level, just like you wouldn't want people to bring you to their level. You have to leave some people behind unfortunately. As they say, "You can't take everyone with you." It will hurt at times, because you want to bring everyone that you can but you can't. This is especially hard for those that are your family members or friends. Some may not think the way that you think. I have learned that some people are comfortable with struggling.

I have been told that I set too many goals or have too many standards. People have called me selfish and self-centered at times because I'm constantly thinking of ways to advance myself. I had to learn that some aren't as ambitious as I am...and I had to become comfortable with that. I prefer to make moves behind the scenes. I don't need accolades for every move or every dollar that I make. That only draws people in to either set you up or try to stay in your pockets. Never let a man or woman be a priority over self. I've always been boy crazy (sarcastically speaking), but I never let it stop me from finishing school, maintaining careers, having assets, and keeping myself together. It feels so damn good to be a movement all your own. There's no need to be a leech from someone else's success.

I'm the person that could be the brainchild behind an event or project, and people wouldn't even know about it. I don't need praise and worship for my every movement. If you don't have a hustler mentality, then you'll never understand a hustler's mentality. I can't stand an ol', "I'm too good to do that type of work" type of person. Don't you know that certain jobs/positions are building blocks for something greater? I'm learning to showcase who I truly am, even if it's not in agreement to what society deems is how I should be. I'll be imperfectly unique in my own way. Continue to speak love and light to those who deserve your energy. Limiting yourself is not an option. Boxing yourself in is not an option. Be set apart from the norm. It's okay to look and be different. Be the change...break the chains.

Some people prefer trash over treasure. The reason is because treasure appears too far in distance in their eyes. Never fear those with the loudest barks. The quietness speaks the loudest volumes. For many years, I've used my personal energy trying to help others get their careers or ventures off the ground. Most of the time, I never asked for a dime. Within recent years, I've seen the same story unfold. They get their business to a comfortable place and then they become distant for no apparent reason. As soon as I see the change up, I change up. I continue to move forward. What I will not do is absorb the rest of my years playing "pretend". I know when a situation isn't genuine. For that, I'll genuinely remove myself from those who want to use, instead of build, a community. I do appreciate those who are true to me and I'll continue to lend a hand to those true people.

"Positive thoughts generate positive feelings and attract positive life experience." - Homean Quotes

Keep Going…Keep Pushing!

I swear that certain life circumstances have turned me into a machine. I think that I've programmed myself to work hard and strive for the best in life. Despite the many challenges that have come my way, I told myself to keep going...to keep pushing. I realize that I don't use my "off" switch nearly as much as I should. I figure that as long as I keep going, then I can try to force the not-so-beautiful things that come my way to be filtered with more beautiful things. I keep allowing love and laughter in as much as possible. I noticed that if I'm not staying busy, then I get trapped in my thoughts. With me being a busy bee, then I am not so focused on the things or thoughts that I so desirably want to go away.

"When you feel like quitting, think about why you started"
– Author Unknown

Stop Allowing People To Abuse Your Time

Time is one of the most valuable things that you can give someone. It is so easy to allow others to absorb your precious time. You have to set limitations on how much time you give out. Time is one of the hardest things to distribute. We want to give our time to our family, friends, work assignments, household chores, time set aside for free time, etc. One thing that helps me with time management is having a handheld planner. I'm actually old school and prefer planners in which I can write in them. I prefer to write and highlight important appointments and meetings. Most people nowadays prefer electronic planning devices. Balancing your time will only be difficult if you allow it to be.

"Small changes will make major impacts in your life."
– Author Unknown

Toni's Keys To a Healthier Body

These consist of sex, herbal teas, vegetarian dishes, bike riding, walking, and lots of laughter. I find that one of the most uncomfortable topics of discussion is sex. Even as adults, a lot of people don't like to discuss it or feel that it's taboo to be brought up. I personally love to talk about sex. It's a part of most of our adulthood. I like to talk about safe and healthy sex. I didn't realize the health benefits of sex until my later adult years. A few things that I learned about sex is that it helps your immune system to fight off certain illnesses. Sex is considered exercise. It is a benefit for men because it lowers their chance of getting prostate cancer. It helps lower your blood pressure. Sex can improve a woman's bladder control. I personally noticed that I had less body aches and pains after I had sex. It was as if my aching joints were less painful and less stiff after I reached an orgasm.

I soon learned of the many benefits of drinking tea. Once I was introduced to herbal teas, I became hooked on them. I noticed that there was a significant change in my appearance. My skin began to have a glow. I soon found that herbal teas were found to be anti-aging. Drinking tea helped prevent me from getting the common cold. The teas were so soothing while I drank it and most certainly helped reduce my stress level. Herbal teas help aid in food digestion. I sometimes had problems with one of my ankles swelling after a foot surgery that I had. When I would drink tea, it helped relieve water pressure, which lessons the pain that was associated. If I was ever feeling down or depressed, some cups of tea helped me feel so much better.

I became pescatarian about six years ago. I began this transition for a better way of living. I read up on the benefits of eating primarily pescatarian, vegetarian, and vegan meals. I pretty much went cold turkey with the transition. It was one of the best decisions that I've ever made. I have had a few cheat meals since, in regards to having poultry. Once I started to incorporate more vegetables and plant-based proteins into my everyday eating, I noticed a significant change in my skin. It most certainly helped with the glowing of my skin. It also improved my digestive system. I realized that vegetarian meals are just as delicious as any of the meals that I've had which included meat.

I've always had a passion for bicycles as much as I love automobiles. I prefer vintage bicycles (or modern bikes that are designed to look vintage) and vintage autos. I started bike riding as an adult several years ago. I wanted to fall back in love with some of my pastime hobbies, which bike riding was on the top of the list. I learned that bike riding was considered a full body workout. It literally works your body from head to toe and it helps with body posture. I also noticed that I as I rode my bike, it lessened the tension that I had on some of my joints. This allowed me to be less tense and more willing to want to ride my bike. My calve and thigh muscles started to look amazing. I've always loved and wanted to have strong beautiful legs. My core muscles started to show form as well. I started to notice my waist getting smaller. Others started to see the transition in my body and the compliments started pouring down on me. I also joined a local bike campaign. It brings awareness to women and helps with building self-esteem by biking. During the spring and summer months, I periodically go bike riding with different bike groups. By riding with these groups, it makes me want to live a healthier lifestyle. The other bike riders were always so positive, which reflected on me and lifted my spirits. With people seeing me ride my bike throughout the community, it gave them the drive to want to ride bikes as well. I believe in encouraging others to want to live a healthy lifestyle. I love being able to help build strong and positive communities. Most importantly, the children in the communities were encouraged to want to ride more along with some of the adults.

Alongside with the bike riding, I decided to incorporate walking more in my everyday living. I have sedentary work assignments, which causes me to have to sit for several hours of the day. Sitting all day puts a toll on my mood and my body. To break up my day and help with my health, I decided to walk during my work breaks. Whenever I have a stressful day, a walk around the city on my breaks really helps. It most certainly helps with my mood. Seeing most people in positive moods while on my walks make a huge difference in my day as well. I walk in any weather (snowy days, rainy days, and warm sunny days). I don't let the change of weather interfere with my walks.

One of my favorite things to do is laugh. I love to make others laugh. Some of my family and friends see me as a comedian. There's no greater feeling than to make someone's day much better. As much as I love to make others laugh, I embrace them making me laugh. It is said that laughter decreases stress and helps release endorphins, which are chemicals in your body that helps you to feel better. It's also said that laughter is considered to be the best medicine. I believe it to be true. Whenever I feel sick or depressed, laughter helps to make any situation much better. If I'm in pain emotionally or physically, laughter relieves most of whatever pain I'm in. With that being said, have lots and lots of sex. Drink many cups of herbal tea. Incorporate bike riding and walking into your life. Also, don't forget to embrace laughter into your lifestyle. Your body will thank you for incorporating all of these things into your life.

"Take care of your body. It's the only place you have to live in."
– Author Unknown

Loving the Life I Live

"Damn right I love the life I live, cause I went from negative to positive and it's all good"- Notorious B.I.G.

I can never express how thankful I am for my life's transition. If you've never lived through the struggles that I've been faced with, then you will never understand. I had so much anger and negativity built up in me. I'm so glad that most of it has been released from me. Being told that I wouldn't be able to do 10% of the things that I've accomplished put a spark in me that's almost unexplainable. One year when I was attending a school conference with my family, my teacher told my mother that I was selfish. At the time, I didn't understand it. When I got home, my mother explained it to me. I was puzzled. I was that student who received honors and helped my classmates often. That also triggered something in me. Even though I realized that my help was unnoticed by one of my teachers, it still didn't change me from wanting to continue to help others. I was sometimes looked at as being naive for believing that people had my best interest. In actuality, a lot of them used me because of my popularity, personal connections, or because of what I was able to give them. I didn't let that deter me from wanting to continue to help others.

I was called "fast", "grown", and "too mature". Some didn't realize that life caused me to have to grow up fast. I didn't lash out at them whenever it was said to me. I used a lot of those moments as tools to help drive me to be amazing. During the days of me celebrating Christmas when I was a child, I used to think that Santa overlooked my siblings and I every year because most of the time it was bare under our tree. Most of the toys that we did receive were from programs or organizations, such as the Santa Claus Girls, Toys For Tots, or even from the few occasions that families would adopt our family for Christmas. It made me dread to see the holidays roll around. Our "fun" times during Christmas celebrations were playing with our cousins and friends' toys. We were so grateful that they were able to share their happiness with us. I was never jealous of them. I was more upset with Santa. Today, I don't celebrate Christmas for my own personal reasons. But there also is no longer anger towards Santa.

"There will always be that one song which brings back all the old memories." *-From "We Need Fun"*

Don't Complain About Being Needed

One day I was having a business meeting. The person that I was meeting with was also someone that I had spoken to about personal things that I had going on. I was telling them how stressful it could be for me with so many people needing me for financial assistance. I mentioned how when I came up on rough times financially, that there weren't many people that I could turn to for help. That person shut me down quick. They said that I was filled with overflow and abundance. They told me that I have more than enough. They mentioned how it was a good thing that people were able to come to me. I was told that it was a blessing that I could be available for so many people. They told me that whenever I need something, I always have a means to get it and how they had never seen me struggle. They said that I was a way maker.

Some people aren't built as strong as I am and some people hope to be as resourceful as I am; I have to remember that. More people want to be able to help others, but they either don't have the means to or don't know how to do so. I was told to not look at the fact that people always need me as a bad or negative thing, but to look at it as only a good thing. It changed my way of looking at certain situations. Even though it can be heavy mentally for me, I know that I'm the greater good of works for other people. When I make others feel good, it bounces back to me. I do feel good when I can help. I also know that I can't make it a habit with helping the same people consistently. It will only hinder them from trying to take care of themselves as well.

"A kind gesture can reach a wound that only compassion can heal." - Steve Maraboli

Ghostwriting

Some years ago, after college, I got into ghostwriting. I actually look at doing that line of work as accidental. Come to think of it, a lot of my work that I've done has been considered accidental. I do also believe that things happen for a reason and that the Creator allows the things that happen in our life. I like to write papers and journal my thoughts. I believe that a person should have more than one line of work. I've seen many people around me lose their jobs without having a backup plan or other flows of income. Because of that, I always made sure that I had a backup plan. Actually, I've always had backups for backups.

I worked for a company that was doing pretty well, as far as revenue coming in for them. One day one of the owners of the business asked if I could write up some promotional work for them. They seemed to be impressed by my work. I was then asked to do more work for them. Their clientele increased drastically. When they noticed the increase in their clientele for business, they asked if I wanted to work on material outside of work. I was told that I could set my own price. At first, I thought it was a gimmick. I had never worked for someone in the past who told me that I could set my own pay. By doing these writing projects for them, I was able to have a more comfortable way of living. Even though the pay that I was receiving was good, the work was very time consuming.

I wanted to continue ghostwriting, but I ended up finding other employment which had even more pay and benefits. I enjoyed my writing projects because I had creative working space. It was a good feeling knowing that I was able to help a business grow as well as helping myself financially. A few people most recently reached out to me to do some more work for them. I was even asked to write a few books for people. I've been contemplating getting back into this line of work. One genre of writing that I've been interested is erotica. So, if I get into anything, erotica writing is going to be next on my list of writing material.

"As a writer you try to listen to what others aren't saying...and write about the silence." - N.R. Hart

Comic Book Character

I had the honor of being made into a comic book character. Someone that I know has been getting themselves prepared to do work in the comic book industry. One day I met up with them and some other family members. We started talking about the different work that we do and side projects that we were involved in. One of the topics that we started talking about was our love for comic books. They proceeded to talk about some of the work that they were involved in as far as comics. I was asked if I wanted to review some of their work. My mind was blown by the work that was put in front of me. I thought to myself how fascinating it would be to be made into a comic character. I mentioned to them that I'd love to be made into a character. From that conversation, they made me inclusive in their work. I was so honored.

For many years, I was into cosplay, and I have dressed up like some of my favorite comic book characters. I would often joke around with people and tell them that I had supernatural powers and that I was a living comic book character. I look forward to seeing my friends' comic book work blossom. I am amazed by what they already have set up. Their future looks so bright and I stand behind them all the way.

"A hero can be anyone. Even a man doing something as simple and reassuring as putting a coat around a little boy's shoulder to let him know that the world hadn't ended." – Batman (The Dark Knight Rises)

2017 End of The Year Reflections

"My main focus for 2017 was to gain closer relationships with my immediate family members. I feel victorious in that area thankfully. I've had to let go of "friendships" that were harmful to my well-being, which wasn't the easiest. They say that you have to pick the thorns from the rose right? Things are looking up in most of the areas of my life. Most of the calendar for 2018 is already filled, so I'm thinking the ride is going to be exciting..."

"I've become prideful when it comes to asking people for help. There are various reasons as to why, but the main reason is because the few times I've asked, I'm either let down or ignored. But...the Creator will put people in your path who are authentic with wanting to help you without you even having to ask and will push you to move and strive. I'm so grateful..."

I decided to share this with you because even though I was making life progress as far back as the year of 2015, when it was a thought to write a book, the following year of 2016 felt as if I went through so much turmoil. In my mind, I felt that the following year would be magical for me, but it was everything but that. There were some highlighting and happy moments, but the majority of the following year of 2016 was so energy draining. I say this because sometimes life just simply doesn't go how we want it to go or expect it go. Regardless of what comes your way, you still have to go through it as gracefully as you possibly can. I'm a believer in speaking life into things, but at times things still don't go as planned. Even with that said, try your best to keep your mental space at peace as much as you can.

"Don't be ashamed of your story. It will inspire others."
– Author Unknown

Some Highlighting Moments During My Writing Process

I rekindled a flame with my husband.

I was asked to model for one of my favorite clothing designers.

I was able to financially pay off a large portion of some personal debts that I had.

I reconnected with some important people from my past.

My skin/hair care products were featured in a boutique in my hometown (Nourish Your Curls Boutique) during their grand opening.

I received some record albums from my family, which dated back many decades ago (they know how much I love music. I also enjoy hosting and attending vinyl music events).

The year prior to my writing process was one of the worst years that I lived through, so to have a year that was the complete opposite was like breathing in crisp fresh air. I breathed clean air into my soul. During this process, it was a mental detox for me. I felt like I was in one of my happiest moments of my life.

"When the student is ready, then the teacher will appear." (When you're ready, the right person will appear in your life)
– Author Unknown

Love on Self and Self Will
Continue to Love on You

I tell people all the time to love on themselves as much as they can. It has nothing to do with arrogance, but all to do with self love and respect. I'm sure that you've noticed that I brought up the topic of self love...a lot. I can't reinforce it enough. I don't see it being done often. It's one of the most important things that we can do for ourselves. When others see us loving on ourselves, they will want to love us even more. I also look at the idea when it comes to business. If I see someone putting effort and love into their business ventures, then I too will want to support them and their business. If you can't march to the beat of your own drum, then why bother trying to strut anyways? March to the beat of your own drum. Own your rhythm. Make your own beat. Don't be afraid to be unique. Don't be afraid to be you.

"If you don't love yourself, you'll always be chasing after people who don't love you either." - Mandy Hale (goodlifequoteru.com)

"Don't compare your life to others. There's no comparison between the sun and the moon. They shine when it's their time."
– From healthyplace.com

A Woman of Comfort Is A Powerful Woman

One of the things that I have noticed when it comes to a man is that they enjoy being in the presence of a woman that will listen to him. It is hard for a man to be vulnerable, emotional, and self-expressive. Sometimes being a listening ear is all he needs. I have siblings, friends, and, of course, my husband who want to vent or get things off their shoulders. No matter what the topic of discussion is, I try to listen openly and with a clear heart and listening ear. It's an emotional battle for men to open up about their insecurities, lacks, true self, and doubts that they feel they have about themselves. I picked up on this many years ago. Some consider men too weak if they do open up about their feelings. If a man does decide to open up to a woman and feel comfortable with doing it, there's so much exchanging of energies. I find women to be powerful if a man is comfortable enough to open up to them. The man sees the woman as having enough strength to take in his emotions and being able to hold them, so the woman in turn is able to hold and uplift him up.

For me, one of the most beautiful things for a man to do is to open up and let me see his full inner self. It takes courage, not even just for a man to do this but for anyone. There is strength in words. So, for someone to be able to hold and take in so much strength, there is power that comes along with it. I'm glad that I can be a woman of comfort to so many people. It's a common thing for me to hear people say, "I love talking to you." It feels good to hear those words. Those words are also a comfort to me as well. Even though I fought moments of violent acts in my life, I was still able to tap into the softer side of myself. I'm glad that people have seen more love than anger in me. I like the softer side of me so much more. The softer side is more tranquil and open to letting love in.

"The beauty of a woman is seen in her eyes, because that is the doorway to her heart, the place where love resides. True beauty in a woman is reflected in her soul. It's the caring that she lovingly gives, the passion that she shows, and the beauty of a woman only grows with passing years." – Audrey Hepburn

Conclusion: Wanting to Leave a Legacy

Why do I share my story? I was told on numerous occasions that I wouldn't be anything in life. I was told that I couldn't possibly be a business owner. I was told that I didn't have the financial stability or drive to even start a business. I was told that I was going to be a product of my environment. I want parents to listen to their children. Some life instances cause children to act out of character. I was told that I was too boy crazy to further my education, where I ended up having six years of college education experience and received a degree and certification. I have a lot of mental and physical scars, but I'm still standing and still smiling on a daily basis. I've learned to turn my hurt into help. I want to show my family, friends, and others that when they are faced with adversity, you can grow and become whatever and whoever you want to be. The city of Grand Rapids has a low success rate in regards to women of color. I wanted to prove that there are strong and intelligent women of color in the city where I was born and raised. I did just that...I proved them wrong.

I have always wanted to leave my mark behind through my artwork. I have a love for all realms of art. I primarily have a passion for photography, body products, painting, reading, and writing. In middle and high school, my passion was writing poetry. I played flute for six years between elementary and high school. One of my biggest regrets was not pursuing a career in music. I would love to be a music producer. I come from a musically-inclined family. I enjoy most genres of music. My favorite era of music is the 1970s. I'm still in love with the vinyl sound.

One of my stress relievers is painting. I have several paintings in my home. I believe that whatever work a person does, it should be celebrated primarily by the one who performs the work. I celebrate my artwork by having it in my home. Once I'm gone from this physical life, people will be able to see a part of me left behind through my work. I intend to leave all of my work to my family. I also make all natural products for the nourishment of the body and hair. The name of my product line is called TONI RAIN All Natural Hair, Body, and Massage Products. I'm currently selling the products

144

from home. Eventually I would like to mass produce, but because I do the mixing, packaging, and delivering, I'm unable to sell on a wider scale. I hope to bring others on board to help build my brand.

Photography is another passion that I have. I love being professionally photographed. My favorite type of photography is Pinup. I'm a lover of almost all things vintage, especially clothing and furniture. I've been modeling locally since the age of 12. Some say that modeling is only for younger generations. I don't agree with that. When you watch commercials or look through magazines, the models vary in age. My feelings are that you're never too young or to old to do what you love to do. Oftentimes, I have been told that I'm naturally photogenic. Posing or "showing face" has always been easy and fun for me.

I loved reading biographies about people growing up and I still do. Years ago it was a thought that I would want someone to learn about me. People tend to gravitate to me. Even though I've struggled with having anger issues, I learned how to let my guard down by pouring love into people. Most people that I come in contact with want to know how I do my makeup, hair, where I purchase my clothes, or just want to know what I have going on in my life. In my younger years, my friends would always want to come to my house to see what I had going on at home or in my neighborhood as well. Even though some of my friends knew about my living situations at home, they still wanted to be under me. I comforted them and they comforted me. With people wanting to know more about me, I figured that the best way would be to put some of my most intimate moments in a book. I've read on several occasions that the best way for self healing is to let it out. I find it to be true for myself. The more I discuss it or open up to people about it, the better I feel. A lot of my life story I was embarrassed about. I had to come to realize that I had to take blame for some of my actions and a lot of the things that took place were out of my control. I had to bring peace to myself and talking about it brought me peace. I felt that I was holding captive in my mind a lot that was bothering me. My only way of releasing it or fixing it was to let others know. Deep down I'm an introvert, but the things that I enjoy doing requires me to have an extroverted lifestyle. I also knew that others have dealt or are maybe still dealing with some of the same issues that I had. I love to love, and I love to help people when I can.

"7 Rules of Life:

1.) Make peace with your past, so it won't screw up the present.

2.) What others think of you is none of your business.

3.) Time heals almost everything, give it time.

4.) Don't compare your life to others and don't judge them. You have no idea what their journey is all about.

5.) Stop thinking too much, it's alright not to know the answers. They will come to you when you least expect it.

6.) No one is in charge of your happiness except you.

7.) Smile. You don't own all the problems in the world."

– From dreamquotes.com

Made in the USA
Columbia, SC
31 January 2019